CorelDRAW
Training Guide

by

Satish Jain

B.Sc., B.E. (II Sc), M.E. (II Sc), M.Tech. (IIT Kanpur),
Ex Professor of Information Technology,
Institute of Information Technology & Management,
GGS Indraprastha University, Delhi.

and

M. Geetha

B.Com., Diploma (IT)

FIRST EDITION 2018
Copyright © BPB Publications, INDIA
ISBN : 978-93-728-400-5

LIMITS OF LIABILITY AND DISCLAIMER OF WARRANTY

Distributors:

BPB PUBLICATIONS
20, Ansari Road, Darya Ganj
New Delhi-110002
Ph: 23254990/23254991

BPB BOOK CENTRE
376 Old Lajpat Rai Market,
Delhi-110006
Ph: 23861747

DECCAN AGENCIES
4-3-329, Bank Street,
Hyderabad-500195
Ph: 24756967/24756400

COMPUTER BOOK CENTRE
12, Shrungar Shopping Centre,
M.G.Road, BENGALURU–560001
Ph: 25587923/25584641

MICRO MEDIA
Shop No. 5, Mahendra Chambers,
150 DN Rd. Next to Capital Cinema,
V.T. (C.S.T.) Station, MUMBAI-400 001
Ph: 22078296/22078297

Published by Manish Jain for BPB Publications, 20, Ansari Road, Darya Ganj, New Delhi- 110002 and Printed him at Repro India Ltd, Mumbai

"Progress is impossible without change; and those who cannot change their mind cannot change anything."

— George Bernard Shaw

Dedicated to

Mata Raj Rajeshwari and Sri Sai Baba

whose blessings overcome all hurdles in life

PREFACE

The objective of this Training Guide is to meet the growing need of the users in exploring CoreDRAW Graphics Suite X8, highly versatile Graphic package in easy-to-understand language. It is observed that most of the books available in the market do not explain CorelDRAW Graphics Suite X8 in step-by-step training manner from the first time user's point of view.

CorelDRAW X8 is a package that enables you to design vector graphics as well as bitmapped graphics at equal ease. Most of the capabilities of this package are explained in this training guide with many illustrations. A very useful feature of this book is that different types of tools in CorelDRAW X8 are explained with practical examples, so as to enable a reader to understand them without any outside help.

Authors

CONTENTS

CHAPTER 1

CorelDRAW Graphics Suite X8 Basics

Introduction

CorelDRAW X8 is a very powerful graphic design package. With that, comes a fairly useful design environment and many combination of tools and effects. In this book you will learn to work with these tools and effects.

Computer graphics programs are classified in two categories. The first types are bitmapped programs like Adobe Photoshop, etc. wherein the images are created in the form of bitmap. The other set of graphic programs use vector graphics where the graphics are composed of mathematical curves. CorelDRAW belongs to the category of vector graphic program. In addition, CorelDRAW X8 comes packaged with Corel PHOTO-PAINT, a powerful image-editing application. You can quickly and easily retouch and enhance image photos.

Before you start creating your own graphic images, you need to understand a few basic concepts about what CorelDRAW X8 does — both on your screen and behind the scenes.

A basic understanding of the unique way in which CorelDRAW creates images will help you to design images and transform those images to print copy or Web page output more effectively.

CorelDRAW X8 is a vector-based program, which means that it creates and handles images as mathematically defined vectors. Vectors are objects with both *magnitude* (size) and *direction* (angles, curvature, and so on). The files that store CorelDRAW X8 images consist of lists of lines, with information on their location, direction, length, colour, and curves.

Note: Defining images as a series of vectors is a more efficient way to work with them than defining images as bitmap or a huge number of individual pixels. This is because even a simple object might have thousands of pixels, each individually defined, whereas the same image might be defined more rationally as a small number of curve segments.

In addition to creating more compact files, CorelDRAW X8's vector-based images have other important advantages. You can easily resize a

CorelDRAW image to a thumbnail sketch or icon or a billboard-sized graphic. When you change the size of a bitmap image, you lose *quality* because the number of dots, or pixels, remains the same even as the illustration is enlarged. That is not the case with CorelDRAW's curve-based illustration. It will not get distorted.

However, graphic designers have to work with bitmaps, especially while working with images that appear in, or as Web pages. Popular Web browsers cannot interpret images created in CorelDRAW's native format. The relatively low resolution of computer monitors tends to negate the advantages of creating vector-based images. The relatively small, low-resolution images seen on Web sites tend to make curves jagged and grainy regardless of how smooth and high-resolution the original image is.

CorelDRAW gives you the capability of creating almost any graphic image file you will ever need. Most of the images are still destined for hard copy, and CorelDRAW's vector-based images are best for printed output. Corel's vector based tools provide the most powerful range of features for designing images. CorelDRAW can then easily translate those images into bitmap formats. In fact, CorelDRAW has a powerful capacity to transform objects into both of the Web-compatible bitmap file format: i.e. GIF and JPEG.

New Features in CorelDRAW Graphics Suite X8

The enhanced layout tools, text improvements, new design assets, redesigned user interface, and improved workflow can boost your productivity and give you a more enjoyable work experience with new features in CorelDRAW X8 help you complete many tasks more easily and in less time.

Optimized for Windows 10 Support: With support for Windows 10, you can confidently use CorelDRAW Graphics Suite X8 on the latest Windows operating system.

New Corel Font Manager: Finally take control of your ever expanding font collection and make the most of the fonts you already handle, and organize your fonts and typefaces quickly. Ideal for professions that use fonts daily, from graphic design, illustration and publishing, to package design, sign making, advertising and website creation.

Enhanced Font Filtering and Search: Quickly find a specific font without spending time searching in multiple folders. For example, search for "script fonts" or a specific character-set and the font list will show all the fonts available.

Enhanced Knife Tool: Split any object or group of objects – vector, text and bitmaps – along straight, freehand or Bézier lines. Overlap objects or create a gap between the new objects after splitting them. Choose an outline option, or let the application automatically select the option that best preserves the outline appearance.

New Design Features Requested by Users: Manage complex projects with ease with the new Hide and Show Objects. Copy, paste, or duplicate pieces of existing curves with Copy Curve and explore the Gaussian Blur to adjust the degree to which the drop shadow feathers at its edges.

New and Enhanced Photo-editing Features: Remove imperfections with the Healing Clone tool and use the enhanced Straighten Image to correct perspective distortions.

New Workspace Customization: Be creative with a workspace that matches your workflow. Alter the desktop and window borders color, select a dark or light UI that suits the way you work, customize the size of text and icons, and open desktop windows within a floating window.

New Learning Tools: Running quickly with a welcoming environment that provides easy setup, in-product learning resources, an improved Hints docker and more.

Enhanced Support for Sharing and Output: The latest standard file formats and design features to create, prepare and deliver your finished document. The advantage of compatibility file formats like AI, PSD, PDF, JPG, PNG, SVG, DWG, DXF, EPS, TIFF, DOCX and PPT. The new Border and Grommet dialog box lets you create a banner from a page or selected objects. Whether you work on small-scale projects, such as logos and web graphics, or larger pieces, such as banners and car wraps, CorelDRAW delivers the output you need.

Minimum System Requirements

- Windows 10, Windows 8.1, or Windows 7 (32-bit or 64-bit editions), with latest updates and service packs.

- Intel Core i3/5/7 or AMD Athlon 64
- 2 GB of RAM
- 1 GB of hard disk space
- 1280 x 720 screen resolution at 100% (96 dpi), 1920 x 1080 at 150%, and 2560 x 1440 at 200%
- DVD drive for installation by disc
- Multi-touch screen, mouse, or tablet
- MS .NET Framework 4.6
- MS Internet Explorer 11 or higher
- Internet connection is required to activate and validate CorelDRAW Graphics Suite, to receive updates, and use online product features and content. The product can be used offline if you connect to the Internet at least once a month to validate your software license.

Getting Started with CorelDRAW Graphics Suite X8

To start CorelDRAW, do this:

1. Click the **Start** menu, highlight **All Programs**, highlight CorelDRAW Graphics Suite X8 and then click on CorelDRAW X8 as shown in Figure 1.1.

Figure 1.1 Starting CorelDRAW Graphics Suit X8

2. The Welcome window appears as shown in Figure 1.2.

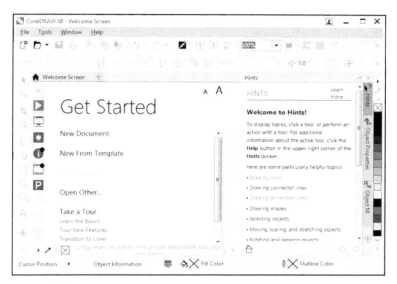

Figure 1.2   Starting with the Welcome Window

CorelDRAW Welcome Screen

The Welcome screen lets you quickly complete common tasks, including the Discovery Center, and lets you quickly complete common tasks, such as opening files and starting files from templates. You can find out about the new features in CorelDRAW Graphics Suite X8 and get inspired by graphic designs featured on the Gallery page. In addition, you can access tutorials and tips, and get the latest product updates as shown in Figure 1.2.

Learning resources

You can learn to use CorelDRAW Graphics Suite X4 in various ways: by reading the user guide; by accessing the Help, Hints, and tooltips; by completing project-based tutorials; and by exploring the resources on the Corel Web site.

Using the Help, Guide and Tooltips

The Help system provides comprehensive information about product features from directly within the program. You can browse through the entire list of topics, check the index, or search the Help for a given word or phrase.

The *CorelDRAW Graphics Suite X8 User Guide* provides information about commonly used product features. The user guide is also available in PDF format and can be accessed through the **Start** menu on the Windows taskbar.

Tooltips provide information about the icons and buttons found in the program. To view a tooltip, position the pointer over an icon, button, or other application control.

Using Hints

Hints provide information about tools in the toolbox from within the application. When you click a tool, a hint appears, telling you how to use the tool. If you need additional information about a tool, you can access a relevant Help topic by clicking the Help button in the upper-right corner of the Hints docker.

Hints are displayed by default in the Hints docker on the right side of the program window, but you can hide them when you don't need them.

Learning Tours

There is a learning tour designed to help you get started quickly. You can take a tour when you start an application or later. Tours are easy to navigate, allowing you to go through consecutive steps or navigate to a specific step.

Accessing eBooks

The CorelDRAW X8 and Corel PHOTO-PAINT X8 user Guide are available as eBooks. Published to the EPUB and MOBI file format.

Video Learning Resources

Two types of video learning resources are available: short videos, known as video hints, and video tutorials.

The short videos show you how to complete basic tasks such as drawing, shaping, and coloring objects in CorelDRAW, or masking and cropping in Corel PHOTO-PAINT. The videos do not have sound, but they provide useful tips and help you understand.

The video tutorials show you how to get the most out of features such as such as font management, fills and transparencies, Content Exchange, alignment tools, QR codes, photo effects, and more.

CorelDRAW Terminology

Before you get started in CorelDRAW X8, you should be familiar with the following terms.

Object An independent element that you can modify. Objects include images, shapes, lines, curves, symbols, text and layers.

Drawing The work you create in CorelDRAW; for example, custom artwork, calendars, posters and newsletters.

Docker window A window containing available commands in a dialog box that remains open as you work.

Flyouts A button which when clicked opens a group of related tools.

List box A list box options that drops down when a user clicks the down arrow button.

Artistic text A type of text to which you can apply special effects, such as shadows.

Paragraph text A type of text that you can use to add blocks of text, which is useful for drawings such as brochures.

Application window

When you launch CorelDRAW, the application window opens containing a drawing window (See Figure 1.3). Although more than one drawing window can be opened, you can apply commands to the active drawing window only.

Toolbox — A floating bar with tools for creating, filling, and modifying objects in the drawing.

Title bar — The area displaying the title of the currently open drawing

Document tab — A tab displays for each document to allow you to quickly move between documents.

Menu bar — The area containing pull-down menu options

Toolbar — It contains shortcuts to menu and other commands

Drawing window — The work you create in CorelDRAW; for example, custom artwork, calendars, posters and newsletters.

Property bar — A commands with that relate to the active tool or object. For example, when the text tool is active, the text property bar displays commands that create and edit text.

Docker window — The area outside the drawing page bordered by the scroll bars and application controls.

Rulers — Horizontal and vertical borders that are used to determine the size and position of objects in a drawing.

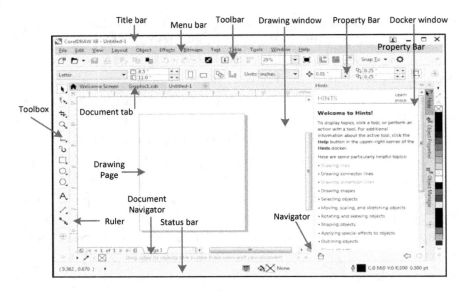

Figure 1.3 CorelDRAW application window

Document navigator—The area at the bottom left of the application window that contains controls for moving between pages and adding pages.

Drawing page—The rectangular area inside the drawing window. It is the printable area of your work area.

Status bar—An area at the bottom of the application window that contains information about object properties such as type, size, color, fill, and resolution. The status bar also shows the current mouse position.

Navigator—A button at the lower-right corner that opens a smaller display to help you move around a drawing.

Color palette—A dockable bar that contains color swatches.

CorelDRAW X8 Interface

A program's interface refers to the way it looks and to the controls, dialog boxes, toolbars, menubar, toolbox, dockers and property bar that enable you interact with it. Figure 1.3 shows the interface of the CorelDRAW X8. It is also called as Application Window. Important parts of this view are shown in Figure 1.3.

Title Bar

The Title bar appears at the top of the CorelDRAW Window. The Title bar shows the name of the file you are currently working on. When the size of the window is less than the maximum size, you can move the entire window by clicking on the title bar and dragging the mouse to a new position.

Menu Bar

The Menu bar is located below the Title Bar and contains the Pull Down Menus. The Pull-down menus contain the CorelDRAW commands. Click on a menu title in the menu bar to pull down the menu.

Toolbox

The toolbox is located to the left of the Drawing window and contains the tools to create and edit graphic objects. When you move the cursor over any of the tools in the toolbox, a ToolTip will appear identifying that tool. Various tools available in the toolbox are explained below in Table 1.1.

Drawing Window

The Drawing window is the whole work area in the middle of your CorelDRAW X8 window, excluding the toolbars, toolbox (on the left), and status bar.

Table 1.1   Tools in Toolbox and their description

Tool	Name	Description
	Pick tool	Lets you select and transform objects.
	Shape tool	The Shape tool lets you edit the shape of objects.
	Crop tool	To cut unwanted areas of an image.
	Zoom tool	The Zoom tool lets you change the magnification level in the Drawing window.
	Freehand tool	The Freehand tool lets you draw lines and curves using mouse.

Tool	Name	Description
↷	Artistic Media Tool	The Artistic media tool provides access to the Preset, Brush, Sprayer, Calligraphic, and Pressure tools.
▢	Rectangle tool	The Rectangle tool lets you draw rectangles and squares.
○	Ellipse tool	Lets you draw ellipses and circles.
⬡	Polygon tool	Lets you draw polygons and stars.
⬡⬜	Basic shapes tool	Lets you choose from a full set of shapes, including hexagram, a smiley face, and a right-angle triangle.
A	Text and Table Tool	Lets you type words directly on the screen as artistic text or a paragraph text. The Table tool lets you draw and edit tables.
⟋	Dimension tools	The dimension tools draw various lines such as slanted, vertical & horizontal, angular, segment and 3-point dimensions.
⌐	Connector tools	This tools draw a straight-line, right-angle, rounded right-angle connector lines and Edit anchor connector line.
⬡	Interactive distortion tool	Lets you apply a Push or Pull distortion, a Zipper distortion, or a Twister distortion to an object.
⟍	Eyedropper tool	This tools lets you select and copy object properties such as line thickness, size and effects from an object.
◈	Interactive fill tool	Lets you apply various fills.
⟁	Outline tool	Opens a flyout that lets you set the outline properties.

Tool	Name	Description
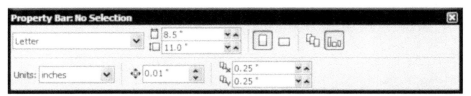	Fill tool	Opens a flyout that lets you set fill properties.

Note: The Drawing window is where you create graphics on the desktop.

Drawing Page

The section of the Drawing window bounded by the shaded box is called the Drawing page. This is the part of the composition that prints when you send a file to the printer.

You can store graphic images that you do not want to print (but do want to save) in the area of the Drawing window outside the Drawing page. The area outside the Drawing page can be a handy storage space when, for example, if you have a file that you use as a template for a publication. You can save logos, blocks of text, etc. for use in another issue of your publication, but they would print if they are not on the Drawing page.

Property Bar

By default the Property Bar sits below the Standard toolbar but you can drag it on any portion of the Property Bar between tools or move it onto the Drawing window. If the Property bar is floating over the Drawing window, you can drag the Property Bar's title bar to move it as per your convenience.

Figure 1.4 Property Bar

The Property Bar gives the information about any selected object in the Drawing window. The Property Bar changes, depending on what object you select in the Drawing window. There is a special Property Bar that appears when you do not have any object(s) selected. In Figure 1.4, because the Drawing window does not have any objects yet, the No selection Property Bar displays information about the Drawing page specification, such as page-size, etc. Note: The Property bar can float over the Drawing window. Moreover, you can dock it just below the Standard toolbar (or on either side or the bottom of Drawing window).

Flyouts

Some tools have a small arrow in the lower left corner. If you click your cursor down on these tools, flyouts appear, and you can transform these tools into any other tools. These flyouts are explained in Table 1.2.

Table 1.2   Flyouts and their Description

Flyout	Description
Shape F10 Smooth Smear Twirl Attract Repel Smudge Roughen Shape edit	Lets you access the Shape, Smudge, Roughen Brush and smooth tools.
Crop Knife Virtual Segment Delete Eraser X Crop tool	Lets you access the Crop, Knife, Eraser and Virtual Segment delete tools.
Zoom Z Pan H Zoom	Lets you access the Zoom and Pan tools.
Freehand F5 2-Point Line Bézier Pen B-Spline Polyline 3-Point Curve Smart Drawing Shift+S Curve	Lets you access the Freehand, Bezier, Artistic media, Pen, Polygon, 3 Point Curve and Smart drawing tool.

☐ Rectangle F6 ⊡ 3-Point Rectangle Rectangle	Lets you access the Rectangle and 3 point rectangle tools.
○ Ellipse F7 ◒ 3-Point Ellipse Ellipse	Lets you access the Ellipse and 3 point ellipse tools.
○ Polygon Y ☆ Star ✿ Complex Star ▤ Graph Paper D ◎ Spiral A ⬚ Basic Shapes ▷ Arrow Shapes ⚑ Flowchart Shapes ▥ Banner Shapes ▱ Callout Shapes Object	Lets you access the Polygon, Star, Complex star, Graph paper and Spiral tools. It also access the Basic shapes, Arrow shapes, Flowchart shapes, Banner shapes and Callout shapes tools.
A Text F8 ▦ Table Text and Table	Let you access **Text** tool lets you type words directly on the screen as artistic or paragraph text. And he **Table** tool draw and edit tables.
✏ Parallel Dimension I⎯ Horizontal or Vertical Dimension ◠ Angular Dimension ʯ Segment Dimension ⌐ 3-Point Callout	Let you access the parallel, horizontal & vertical dimension, angular dimension, and segment dimensions and 3-point callout.
➹ Straight-Line Connector ➷ Right-Angle Connector ➷ Rounded Right-Angle Connector ⌑ Edit Anchor	Let you access the straight-line, right-angle and rounded right-angle connector and Edit anchor tools.
⬚ Drop Shadow ◻ Contour ❀ Blend ◰ Distort ✕ Envelope ✤ Extrude Interactive tools	Lets you access the Interactive blend, Interactive contour, Interactive distortion, Interactive drop shadow, Interactive envelope, Interactive extrude, and Interactive transparency tools.

Color Eyedropper **Attributes Eyedropper** Eyedropper tool	Lets you access the Eyedropper and Attributes Eyedropper tools.
Outline Pen F12 Outline Color Shift+F12 No Outline Hairline Outline 0.5 pt 0.75 pt 1 pt 1.5 pt 2 pt 3 pt 4 pt 8 pt 10 pt Outline tool	Lets you access an Outline pen dialog, Outline color dialog, Color Docker window, Hairline Outline and a selection of outline of various widths.
Interactive Fill G Mesh Fill M Interact ive tool	Lets you access Interactive fill and Interactive mesh fill tools.

Standard Toolbar

The Standard toolbar is directly under the Menu bar, and it displays icons for commands like New, Open, Save, Print, Copy, and Paste.

The Standard tools in toolbar are always available, but you can display additional tools as well.

Along with the Standard toolbar, CorelDRAW X4 activates interactive Property Bar when you select different types of objects. For example, if you select a shape, the Shape Property Bar appears under the Standard toolbar. If you select a text frame, the Text Property Bar becomes active. The elements of the Standard toolbar are explained in Table 1.3.

Table 1.3   Tools on the Standard toolbar

Tool	Tool Name	What It Does?
	New	Opens a new file.
	Open	Activates the Open Drawing dialog box so you can open an existing file.

Tool	Tool Name	What It Does?
	Save	Resaved an already saved file, or opens the Save Drawing dialog box.
	Print	Print a drawing.
	Cut	Cuts selected objects and places them in the Clipboard, from which they can be pasted.
	Copy	Copies selected objects into the Clipboard.
	Paste	Pastes the contents of the Clipboard into the Drawing area.
	Undo	The icon undoes your last action; the drop-down list enables you to undo a series of actions.
	Redo	The icon redoes the last undone action; the drop-down list enables you to redo multiple undo actions.
	Search content	Display search for content such as clipart, photos, fonts, and more.
	Import	Opens the Import dialog box from which you can import non-CorelDRAW files.
	Export	Opens the Export dialog box. Enabling you to export objects or files to other file formats.
PDF	Publish to PDF	Export to the document to the pdf file format.
51%	Zoom levels	The drop-down list enables you to zoom in or zoom out on your drawing.

Tool	Tool Name	What It Does?
■	Display Full-screen preview	Shows the full screen preview of the document.
	Show rulers	Show or hide rulers
	Show grid	Show or hide grid
	Show guidelines	Show or hide guidelines
Snap to ▾	Snap To	Select the method for aligning objects on the page.
⚙	Options	Open the Options dialog box

Note: Toolbars stay on the screen until you turn them off, and Property Bars appear or disappear depending on what objects you select.

Controlling the display of Toolbars

You can move toolbars onto the Drawing page, or dock them under the Standard toolbar. If you do not want the Property Bar to appear, right-click on it, and uncheck Property Bar from the context menu.

To control the display of Toolbars do this:

1. Right-click the Standard toolbar or the current Property Bar. A list of toolbars appears.

2. Click on the toolbar from the context menu you want to display. A toolbar is displayed when a check mark appears against the toolbar, as shown in Figure 1.5. Or

3. To toggle between displaying and hiding a toolbar, click **Window** menu and choose **Toolbars**, and click the command with the toolbar name.

To dock a toolbar do this:

1. Click the toolbar border, and drag the toolbar to the edge of the application window until it changes shape.

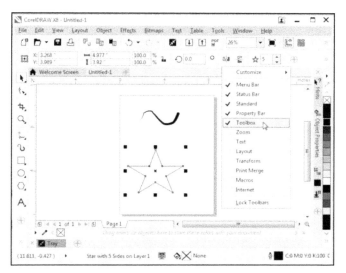

Figure 1.5 Checking text from Context menu to display the Toolbox

2. Release the mouse button to dock the toolbar.

To float a toolbar do this:

1. Click on a section of the toolbar between tools (not on a tool).

2. Drag the toolbar into the Drawing area.

Working with Docker Windows

Docker windows are similar to conventional dialog boxes, but are more interactive. They remain on the screen, until you close them. They can be placed next to the object you are drawing. This provides quick access to the commands placed in the docker window and their subsequent execution. Dockers can be either docked or floating. Docking a toolbar attaches it to the edge of the application window. Undocking a docker detaches it from other parts of the workspace; so it can be easily placed wherever you want.

To see a list of Dockers available in the Dockers sub menu do this:

1. Click Windows menu, highlight Dockers as shown in Figure 1.6.

To dock a floating docker, do this:

1. Drag the docker's title bar or tab to an edge of the drawing window and position the pointer along the edge. When a grey preview of the docker's position appears, release the mouse button.

CorelDRAW Graphics Suite X8 Basics   **17**

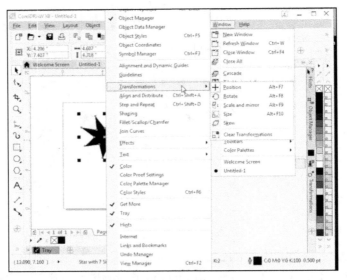

Figure 1.6 List of Dockers

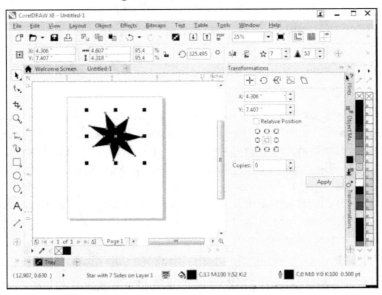

Figure 1.7 Applying position in docker window

In Figure 1.7, you see Transformations Docker window available in CorelDRAW, which enables you to position the object. Disable the Relative Position check box in the Transformation docker. Type the value in the X: and Y: list box and then click Apply button.

The Status Bar

The Status bar is located below the Drawing area and gives you important information about a selected object. The status bar tells you the type of object you have selected and the type of fill. For example, in Figure 1.7, the status bar show that the object selected is a Star with 7 slides and that the fill color is Red. This is very useful when your illustration involves hundreds of objects. The status bar is a handy way to tell exactly what object is selected.

The status bar identifies the location of the cursor in x and y coordinates on the left side of the screen.

- The x value (the first one) represents the distance from the left edge of the Drawing page.
- The y value (the second one) represents the distance your current point is from the bottom of the Drawing page.

The Status bar also tells you what layer you are working with. (Complex Corel DRAW files can have more than one layer). (See Figure 1.8)

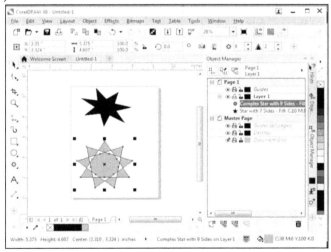

Figure 1.8 Status Bar elements

CorelDRAW View

You can control how you see and work with a page by selecting from six view options. CorelDRAW objects take quite a bit of system resources. When you fill a screen with objects, editing can be slow.

Lower quality views can speed up that process. View quality settings from lowest to highest are:

- **Simple Wireframe**–It displays an outline of the drawing by hiding fills, extrusions, contours, drop shadows, and intermediate blend shapes. It also displays the bitmapped images in monochrome.
- **Wireframe**–It displays an outline of the drawing by hiding fills only.
- **Draft**–It displays a drawing's fills and bitmapped images using a low resolution.
- **Normal**–It displays the drawing without postscript fills and without high-resolution bitmapped images.
- **Enhanced**–It displays the drawing with postscript fills and high resolution.
- **Simulate overprints**–It simulates the color of areas where overlapping objects were set to overprint and displays PostScript fills, high-resolution bitmaps, and anti-aliased vector graphics.
- **Rasterize complex effects**–Rasterizes the display of complex effects, such as transparencies, bevels, and drop shadows when in Enhanced view. This option is useful for previewing how the complex effects will be printed.

Figures 1.9 to 1.11 show the three different views of the same drawing. The view you select affects the time it takes to open or refresh a drawing.

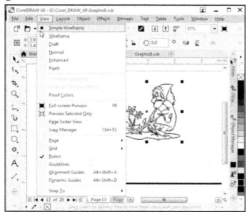

Figure 1.9   Simple Wireframe does not show the color fills

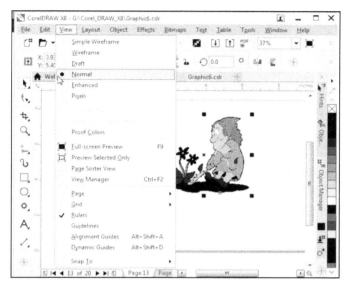

Figure 1.10 Normal view shows fills with low resolution

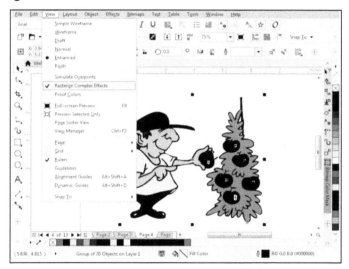

Figure 1.11 Display of Rasterize complex effects

For example, a drawing in Simple Wireframe view opens or refreshes in less time than a drawing in enhanced view.

With CorelDRAW X8, enhanced view has become the default view setting. Enhanced view does provide a cleaner, less sharp picture of an illustration, but it is also slower to reflect drawing changes than Normal view. Depending on your PC hardware type and main memory in it, you can experiment by using Normal view. When you are working with pictures that slow your screen resolution, work in Draft view, and even Wireframe view if possible.

Zooming and Panning

You can zoom in and out in CorelDRAW, and use the Pan (hand) tool to drag parts of a drawing into the viewable window. The Zoom tool works as an interactive magnifying glass enabling you to focus on a small part of your page or zoom out to see the entire Drawing area. You can select different zoom magnifications.

To set different values of zoom do this:

1. Click the **Zoom** level from the Zoom Levels drop-down list in the Standard toolbar as shown in Figure 1.12.

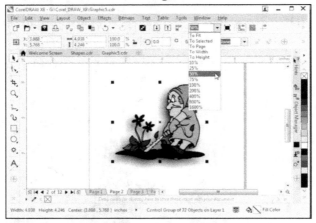

Figure 1.12 Zoom levels in the standard toolbar

2. *Alternatively*, you can zoom in and out interactively by clicking on the Zoom tool in the toolbox and then clicking on a portion of your drawing that you want to magnify.

3. Or you can Zoom back out by pressing the **F3** function key on your keyboard.

4. The Zoom tool in the Toolbox is a flyout, and when you click on it and hold down the mouse button, you can choose between the Zoom tool and the Hand tool. Or

5. Click on the Property bar, choose one of the following buttons and observe the effect on the display and on the percentage magnification. (See Figure 1.13)

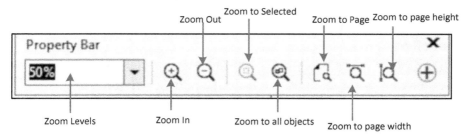

Figure 1.13   Zoom Tool property bar

To zoom using keyboard shortcuts, do this:

1. To zoom in, press Ctrl + (+) plus sign keys together.
2. To zoom out, press Ctrl + (-) minus sign keys together.

The Pan tool enables you to click on a section of an image and drag that section of the image into view. The Pan tool cursor looks like a hand, and the Zoom tool cursor looks like a magnifying glass.

To use the Pan tool do this:

1. Open the Zoom flyout, and click the Hand tool. (See Figure 1.14)
2. Drag in the Drawing window until the area you want to view is displayed.
3. To pan in the drawing window while zoomed in on the drawing, click the Navigator button ⊙ in the lower-right corner of the drawing window.

To scroll by using a mouse wheel, do this:

1. To scroll vertically, press Alt key while you move the wheel.
2. To scroll horizontally, press Ctrl key while you move the wheel.

Note: The Pan and Zoom tools have no effect on the actual appearance of your finished image; they simply enable you to view images from different perspectives.

CHAPTER 2

Basic Drawing

Introduction

CorelDRAW X8 has different shape tools that you use to create lines, ellipses, circles, and rectangles including squares, polygons and stars. Shape tools have their own rules in CorelDRAW. In this chapter, you will learn to draw *lines, curves,* etc. using shape tools. Although CorelDRAW X8 has numerous effects and combinations of effects, most graphic designs boil down to combinations of shapes and text.

Working with Lines

A line is a path between two points. Lines can consist of multiple segments, and the line segments can be curved or straight. The line segments are connected by nodes, which are depicted as small squares. CorelDRAW provides various drawing tools that let you draw curved and straight lines, and lines containing both curved and straight segments.

Lines are the basic unit of almost all drawings. Therefore, you should first experiment with drawing lines before moving on to draw complex shapes.

CorelDRAW X8 lets you draw different types of lines. These are *straight lines, freehand lines, calligraphic lines* and *Bezier lines.*

To draw a straight line, do this:

1. Click the Curve flyout from the toolbox, and choose the Freehand tool.

2. Click in the drawing window where you want to start the line. Now, click at a point, where you want to end it. A straight line will be formed joining these two points (See Figure 2.1).

3. Using **Ctrl** key you can draw straight line angles in increments of 15°. That is you can draw straight lines at angles 0°, 15°, 30°, 45°, 60° and 90°, etc. This is useful for drawing *horizontal, vertical* and *straight* lines. After choosing the starting point, hold down **Ctrl** key. Now you will observe that the end point can be chosen only at the above particular angles. After pressing the **Ctrl** key, you cannot select end point at your will.

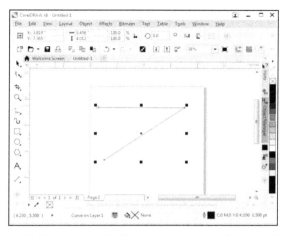

Figure 2.1   A straight line drawn using freehand tool

To Reposition a line, do this:

1. Hold down both the left and right mouse buttons, and drag the line to new position.
2. To add a line segments to an existing line, click the end node of a selected line, and click where you want the new segment to end.

Drawing a Curve

CorelDRAW X8 gives you many options to draw curves. Freehand curve are the simplest of them all. Therefore, you will first learn to draw these.

Note: Freehand curve got its name because it looks much like a hand drawn curve.

To draw a freehand curve, do this:

1. Click the Curve flyout, and choose the Freehand tool. Click and hold down left mouse button drag across the drawing page. You can draw a curve as you want it. (See Figure 2.2).
2. To draw a symmetrical curve, hold the **Shift** key while dragging.

Bezier Lines and Curves

A line which is drawn one segment at a time by adding nodes are called Bezier lines. These lines can be drawn with the Bezier tool. Bezier lines and curves contain many nodes or control points. These nodes can be manipulated, dragged or pulled to draw the shape you want. Thus, the advantage with Bezier lines and curves lies in the fact that they can be modified after drawing them.

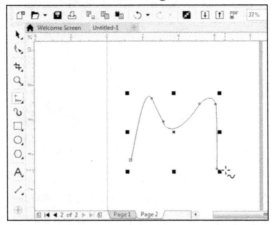

Figure 2.2   M shaped curved line drawn with freehand tool

To draw a Bezier line, do this:

1. Click the **Curve** flyout from the toolbox, and choose the **Bezier** tool.

2. Click where you want to start the line and draw lines with multiple segments by using the Bézier tool and clicking each time you want the line to change direction. (See Figure 2.3)

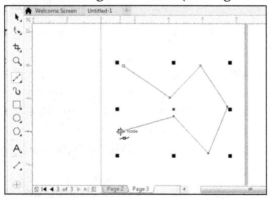

Figure 2.3   Drawing a Bezier line

To draw a Bezier curve do this:

1. Click the **Curve** flyout and choose **Bezier** tool.

2. To draw a curved segment, click where you want to place the first node, and drag the control handle to where you want to place the next node. Release the mouse button, and drag the control handle to create the curve.

3. Try to make a drawing, using Bezier tool, like the one shown in Figure 2.4.

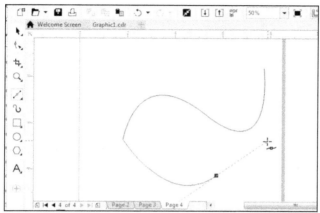

Figure 2.4 Bezier Curve draw

B-spline tool

By using control points, you can easily shape a curved line and draw B-splines, which are typically smooth, continuous curved lines. B-splines touch the first and last control points and are pulled by the points in between. The control points that touch the line are referred to as "clamped."

To draw a curve using Pen tool do this:

1. In the toolbox, click the **B-spline** tool.
2. Click where you want to start the line.
3. Click to set as many control points as you need to shape your line. Control points float by default, but you can clamp control points to the line by pressing **V** while clicking. (See Figure 2.5).
4. Double-click to finish the line.

Drawing Curve Using Pen Tool

To draw a curve using Pen tool do this:

1. Open the Curve flyout and click the Pen tool.

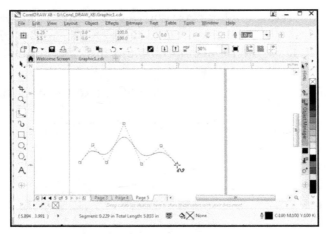

Figure 2.5   Using the B-spline tool to set the control point

2. Click where you want to place the first node, and drag the control point in the direction you want the curve to bend.
3. Release the mouse button. Position the cursor where you want to place the next node, and drag the control point to create the curve you want (See Figure 2.6).
4. Double-click to finish the curve.

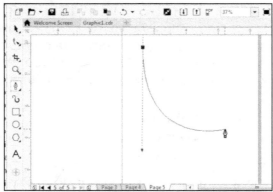

Figure 2.6   Curve using Pen tool

Drawing a line by Using Polyline Tool

To draw a line by using Polyline tool do this:

1. Open the Curve flyout, and click the Polyline tool. Click where you want to start the straight line, and then click where you want to end it.

2. To draw a curve, click where you want to start the curve, and drag across the drawing page.

3. Double-click to finish the curve.

To draw an arc by using Polyline tool do this:

1. Click the Polyline tool.

2. Click in the drawing window, and then release the mouse button.

3. Hold the Alt key and move the pointer to create an arc.

4. Double-click to finish the arc as shown in Figure 2.7.

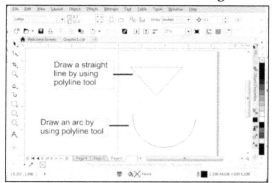

Figure 2.7 Using Polyline tool by using straight line and an arc

Drawing Curve Using 3-Point Curve Tool

To draw a curve using 3-Point Curve tool do this:

1. Open the Curve flyout, and click the 3 point curve tool.

2. Click where you want to start the curve, and drag to where you want to curve to end.

3. Release the mouse button, and click where you want the center of the curve to be. (See Figure 2.8)

Rectangles and Squares

Rectangles and squares are the basic shapes available with most drawing software packages. CorelDRAW X8 lets you draw rectangles and squares with great ease.

To draw a rectangle, do this:

Using Rectangle Tool

1. Open the Rectangle flyout and then click the Rectangle tool.

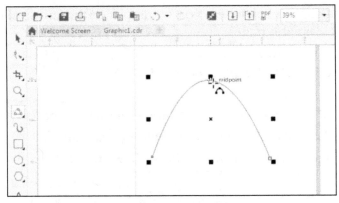

Figure 2.8   Curve using 3-point Polyline tool

Move the cursor to the first point of the rectangle and click. Now drag in the drawing window until the rectangle is of the size you want. (See Figure 2.9)

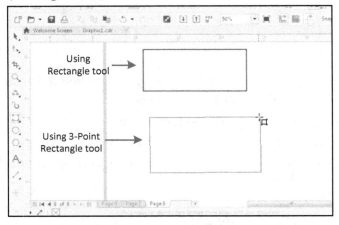

Figure 2.9   Different types of Rectangles

2. *Alternatively*, you can draw a rectangle that covers the drawing page by double-clicking the Rectangle tool.

Using 3 Point Rectangle Tool

1. Open the **Rectangle** flyout, and click the **3-Point Rectangle** tool.

2. In the drawing window, point to where you want to start the baseline of the rectangle, drag to draw the width, and release the mouse button (See Figure 2.9).

3. Move the pointer to draw the height, and click. To adjust the size of the rectangle, type values in the Object size boxes on the property bar.

Note: To constrain the angle of the baseline to a preset increment, known as constrain angle, hold down Ctrl as you drag.

To draw a square do this:

Using Rectangle Tool

1. Open the **Rectangle** flyout and then click the **Rectangle** tool.
2. Press and hold down **Ctrl** key and drag diagonally the rectangle tool in the drawing window. Continue dragging until the Square is of the size you want (See Figure 2.10).

Using 3 Point Rectangle Tool

1. Open the **Rectangle** flyout, and click the **3-Point Rectangle** tool.
2. In the drawing window, point to where you want to start the square, drag to draw the width, and release the mouse button (See Figure 2.10).
3. Move the pointer while holding **Ctrl** key and click.

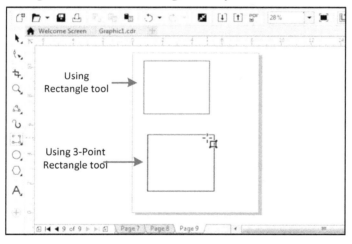

Figure 2.10 Different types of Squares

*Note: You can draw a rectangle from its center outward by holding down **Shift** as you drag. You can also draw a square from its center outward by holding down **Shift + Ctrl** as you drag.*

Ellipses and Circles

Ellipses also known as ovals can be drawn in CorelDRAW X8 using the *Ellipse* tool from the Toolbox.

To draw an ellipses do this:

Using Ellipse Tool

1. Open the Ellipse flyout, and click the Ellipse tool, and drag in the drawing window until the ellipse is of the shape you want (See Figure 2.11). The ellipse will continue to grow in size until you release the mouse button.

2. To draw an ellipse from the centre to outward, hold down the Shift key while you drag.

Using 3 Point Ellipse Tool

1. Open the **Ellipse** flyout, and click the **3-Point Ellipse** tool.

2. In the drawing window, point to where you want to start the ellipse. Drag to draw the centerline, and release the mouse button. (See Figure 2.11)

3. Move the pointer to draw the height, and click.

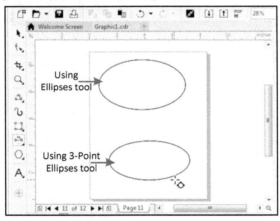

Figure 2.11 Different Types of Ellipses

To draw a circle, do this:

Using Ellipse Tool

1. Open the Ellipse flyout, and click the Ellipse tool, press and hold down Ctrl key, and drag in the drawing window until the Circle is of the size you want (See Figure 2.12).

2. To draw a circle from the centre to outward, hold down the **Ctrl + Shift** keys together while you drag.

Using 3-Point Ellipse Tool

1. Open the **Ellipse** flyout, and click the **3-Point Ellipse** tool.
2. In the drawing window, point to where you want to start the circle, drag to draw the centerline, and release the mouse button (See Figure 2.12).
3. Move the pointer while holding **Ctrl** key, and click.

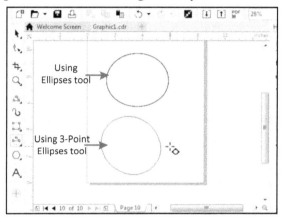

Figure 2.12 Different Types of Circles

Polygons and Stars

A Polygon is any closed figure with 3 or more sides. In CorelDRAW X8, you can draw polygons of any number of sides using the polygon tool. This tool also allows you to draw stars or polygon as stars.

To draw a polygon, do this:

1. Click the **Polygon** tool and drag in the drawing window until the polygon is of the size you want (See Figure 2.13). By default, the polygon drawn is a pentagon.
2. In order to draw polygons other than pentagon, change the number of sides of polygon, type a value in the *points* or *sides* box in the Property bar.
3. To draw a polygon from centre to outward hold down **Shift** key as you drag.
4. To draw a symmetrical polygon hold down **Ctrl** key as you drag.

To create a Star, do this:

1. Click the **Star** tool and drag in the drawing window until the star is of the size you want (See Figure 2.13).

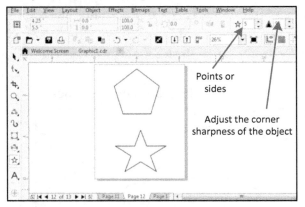

Points or sides

Adjust the corner sharpness of the object

Figure 2.13 Drawing a Polygon and a Star

2. To draw a star from centre to outward, hold down **Shift** key as you drag.
3. To draw a symmetrical star press and hold down **Ctrl** key as you drag.
4. To adjust the number of sides or points on a selected star, type a value in the **sides or points** box on the Property bar.
5. To adjust the sharpness on a selected star, type a value in the **Sharpness** box on the Property bar.

Selection Techniques

Before you can change an object, you must select it. You can select visible objects, hidden objects, and a single object in a group or a nested group. You can also select multiple objects all at once. You can also select objects in the order in which they were created.

To select objects do this:

1. Click **Pick** tool from the toolbox. Then click on the object with it. Or
2. To select many objects at once, hold down **Shift** key, and click each object you want to select. Or
3. To select all objects in the Drawing area, click the <u>E</u>dit menu and choose Select <u>A</u>ll <u>O</u>bjects.

4. To select an object, starting with the first object created and moving toward the last object created, Press **Shift + Tab** keys together until a selection box displays around the object you want to select. Or

5. To select an object, starting with the last object created and moving toward the first object created, press **Tab** key until a selection box displays around the object you want to select.

To deselect already selected object(s) do this:

1. To deselect a single object click with the **Pick** tool a blank space in the drawing window.

2. To deselect a single object in multiple selected objects, press and hold down **Shift** key and click the object using the **Pick** tool.

Using Rulers

Rulers are the measuring tools displayed on the *left* side and along the *top* of the drawing window. The rulers help you size and position the objects in your drawing.

Rulers can help you *size, align* and *draw* objects accurately. You can hide the rulers or move them to another position in the drawing window. You can also customize the ruler settings to suit your needs. For example, you can set the ruler origin and select a unit of measure.

To control the display of rulers do this:

1. Click the <u>V</u>iew menu and choose <u>R</u>ulers. The ruler is displayed when a check mark appears.

2. To hide the ruler click again.

When you move any object, you can see a white dotted line on the left and top rulers. These lines help you to position your object correctly.

To customize ruler settings do this:

1. Click T<u>o</u>ols menu and choose <u>O</u>ptions... . You will find that Options Dialog box appears. Alternatively, you can press **Ctrl+J**.

2. In Options dialog box, click **Document** list of categories as shown in Figure 2.14. *Alternatively*, the options dialog box can also be opened by double clicking anywhere on the rulers.

3. The **Nudge:** This specifies how far the object moves when you press **up, down, right** or **left** arrow key. For example, if you set

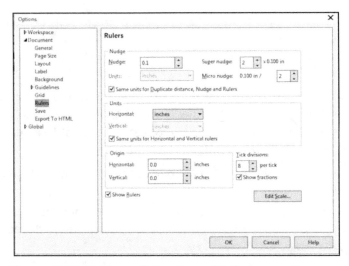

Figure 2.14 Options dialog box with Rulers options

Nudge to 1 inch and choose the object using **Pick** tool, then if you press **down** arrow key, the object will move 1 inch down.

4. To set units of measurements for the placement of duplicate objects and nudge values different from that of ruler units, uncheck the **Same units for Duplicate distance**, **Nudge** (move an object in increment) **and Rulers** check box.

5. In the **Units** area, choose a unit of measure from the **Horizontal**: list box.

Note: Duplicate objects are created by pressing **Ctrl+D** *keys together. Alternatively, duplicate objects can be created by clicking* **E**dit *menu and then choosing* **D**uplicate.

6. To set different units of measurements for the Vertical and Horizontal rulers, uncheck the **Same units for Horizontal and Vertical rulers** check box, and then type the values in the **Horizontal**: and **Vertical**: list box.

7. In the **Origin** area, type values for the origin in the **Horizontal**: and **Vertical**: list box.

8. To divide a unit into a fixed number of sub divisions other than the default value, type a value in the **Tick divisions** box.

9. Uncheck or check **Show Rulers** check box to show/hide rulers.

To move rulers, do this:

1. Hold down Shift Key
2. Drag the rulers to the desired position

Using Grids and Guidelines

Grids and guidelines are tools that enable you to easily position a selected object to a horizontal or vertical location, or both.

Working with the grid displayed is like working on graph paper. You can use grids to align an object to a position. The grids are not printed. Similarly, guidelines are non-printing lines placed to align and place the objects in your drawing. Guidelines are of two types, vertical and horizontal. Figure 2.15 shows a horizontal and a vertical guideline.

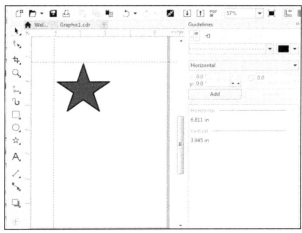

Figure 2.15 Horizontal and vertical guideline

You can have objects snap to the guidelines, so that when an object is moved near a guideline, it can only be centered on the guideline or lined up on either side of the guideline.

Snap to Grid feature will make the grid coordinates act like magnets that attract the object you are moving. If you want to move an object to a location not on a grid coordinate, you will find it difficult with Snap to Grid turned on.

Finally, you can place custom-defined horizontal and vertical guidelines on your page and use them to align objects to a required position.

Note: The hotkey for toggling Snap to Grid on and off is Ctrl+Y.

To display or hide guidelines, do this:

1. Click View menu and choose Guidelines.

2. A check mark beside the Guidelines command indicates that the guidelines are displayed.

Note: You can also display or hide the guidelines by clicking Windows menu highlight Dockers and then choose Guidelines and clicking the Show or hide guidelines button

To add a horizontal or vertical guideline, do this:

1. Click Window menu highlight Dockers and choose Guidelines.

2. Choose one of the following options from the Guideline type list box:

   • Horizontal or Vertical

3. To add an angled guideline, choose Angled from the **Guideline type** list box.

4. Specify the location of the guideline in the **x:** and **y:** box.

5. Type a value in **Angle of rotation** box.

6. Click Add as shown in Figure 2.15.

You can also add a guideline by dragging from the horizontal and vertical ruler to the drawing window.

To set snapping, options dialog box, do this:

1. Drag on the ruler (on the left side for vertical guideline or top for horizontal guideline) of the Drawing window, and pull it to the position you want to place the guide.

2. Click Window menu and choose Options.... . The Options dialog box appears as in Figure 2.16.

3. Click Document categories a list of options appears, click Guides. The Guides options appear at the right side.

4. In the dialog box, click the Vertical or Horizontal as per your need.

5. Specify the setting you want.

6. Click Add button.

7. If you clear the guidelines, click the **Clear** button.

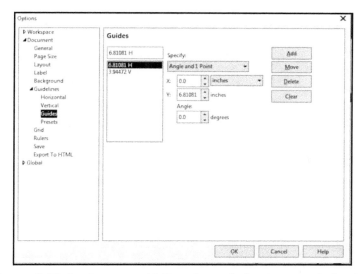

Figure 2.16 Setting up guideline through the Options dialog box

Snap to Guidelines

Snap to guidelines features, when turned on, makes the guidelines behave like magnets. That is when you move the object near the guidelines it sticks to the guideline.

To snap to guidelines do this:

1. Click the Vi̲ew menu highlight Snap to and choose Guidelines. Now the guidelines will act as magnetic borders.
2. Drag the object to the guideline.
3. To snap the center of an object to a guideline, select the object, and drag it by its center over the guideline until the center snaps to the guideline as shown in Figure 2.17.

To remove guidelines, do this:

1. Select the guideline you want to remove with the Pick tool.
2. Press the Delete button.

CorelDRAW X8 allows you to snap the objects. That is, you can force an object that is being drawn to align automatically to a point on another object.

Snap to Objects

Snap to object means to force an object to align automatically to a

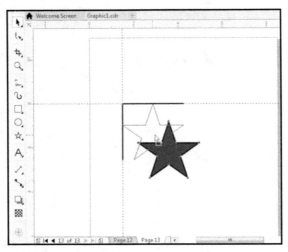

Figure 2.17 Snap to center of an object to a guideline

point on the grid, a guideline, or another object. You can snap an object to a number of snap points in the target object. When the pointer is close to a snap point, the snap point is highlighted, indicating it as the target that the pointer will snap to. For example, you can snap the pointer to a rectangle's center, and then drag the rectangle by its center and snap it to the center of another rectangle.

To customize snap to objects, do this:

1. Click on <u>T</u>ools menu and choose <u>O</u>ptions... . The Options dialog box appears.

2. Click Workspace options from the list and select Snap to Objects.

3. In the Right side **Snap to Objects** options are appears as shown in Figure 2.18.

4. In the *Snapping modes* area, enable one or more of the mode check boxes on or off.

5. If you want to enable all snapping modes, click **Select all**.

6. If you want to disable all snapping modes, but without turning off snapping, click **Deselect all**.

7. Display or hide snapping mode indicators, Enable or disable the **Show snap location marks** check box.

8. Display or hide screen tips, Enable or disable the **Screen Tip** check box.

9. Choose one or more tasks to turn snapping on or off

- Enable snapping for all objects, click **View** menu highlight **Snap To** and choose **O**bjects.

- Enable snapping objects to page elements (edges, edge midpoints, and page center) click **View** menu highlight **Snap To** and choose **Page.**

- Enable snapping objects to the pixel grid click **View** menu highlight **Snap To** and choose **Pixels.** This option is available only when pixel view is enabled.

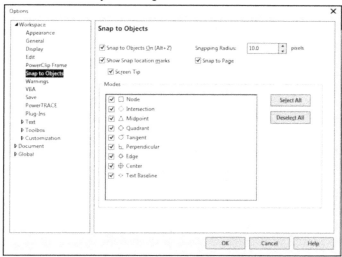

Figure 2.18 Customizing Snapping Objects

To snap to Objects do this:

1. Select the objects.

2. Click **V**iew menu **Snap To** and choose **O**bjects. Or Alternatively Click **Alt+Z** keys together.

3. Move the object using **Pick** tool. You will observe that the object will appear to be magnetized and stick tightly to the other objects (See Figure 2.19).

Using Dynamic Guides

Dynamic guides help you to precisely move, align, and draw objects relative to other objects. These guides are temporary guidelines that

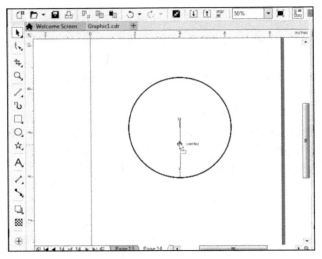

Figure 2.19 Snap Arrow to Circle

you can pull from the following snap points in objects — center, node, quadrant, and text baseline.

When you drag an object along a dynamic guide, you can view the object's distance from the snap point used to create the dynamic guide, and place the object precisely. The screen tip displays the angle of the dynamic guide and the distance between the node and the pointer. Dynamic guides contain invisible divisions called ticks to which your pointer moves. Ticks let you move objects with precision along a dynamic guide. You can also set other options for dynamic guides. For example, you can choose to display dynamic guides at one or more preset angles, or at custom angles you specify.

To display dynamic guides do this:

1. Click <u>V</u>iew and choose D<u>y</u>namic Guides. Or *Alternatively* Click Alt + Shift + D keys together.

2. Click on a drawing tool which you create.

3. Move the pointer over and then off an eligible snap point of an object.

4. Drag the object to an eligible snap point of the target object.

5. When the snap point of the target object becomes highlighted, drag the object along the dynamic guide to position it. (See Figure 2.20)

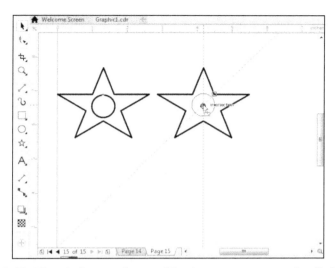

Figure 2.20 The circle was dragged by its center snap point (left) to the
intersection of the other object

*Note: To avoid displaying too many dynamic guides, you can clear the queue
of points at any time by pressing Esc key.*

To set options for dynamic guide, do this:

1. Click <u>W</u>indow menu highlight <u>D</u>ockers and choose **Alignment and
   Dynamic <u>G</u>uides**. The Dockers window appears as shown in
   Figure 2.21.

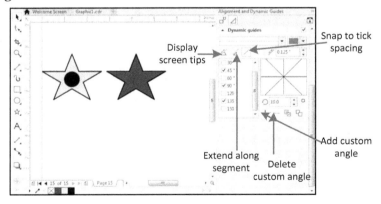

Figure 2.21 Set options for dynamic guides

2. Select the **Line style** picker, and choose a line style, to change the
   line style of dynamic guides.

3. Select the **Line color** picker, and choose a color, to change the color of dynamic guides.

4. Click on Distance screen tips button to display or hide the angle of dynamic guides and the distance from the snap point used to create the dynamic guide.

5. Click the **Extend along segment** button to display dynamic guides that are extensions of line segments.

6. Click the **Snap to tick spacing** button and type a value in the Tick spacing box to snap the invisible divisions on the dynamic guides.

7. Enable or disable the angle check boxes to choose the angles at which to create the dynamic guides.

8. Type a value in the **Custom angle** box, and click the **Add custom angle** button to add a custom dynamic guide angle.

9. Select a dynamic guide in the list, and click the **Delete custom angle** button to Delete a dynamic guide angle.

10. To select all angles given in Guides area Select All button.

11. If you do not want to show the dynamic guides on the predefined angles you can deselect them by pressing Deselect All button.

Defining Grids

To display grids do this:

1. Click View menu highlight Grid and choose Document Grid.

2. A check mark beside the **Document grid** command indicates that the document grid is displayed.

3. You can also adjust the distance between the grids. Also the frequency, i.e. the number of lines between each vertical and horizontal unit, can be set according to your requirement. The intersecting horizontal and vertical lines are called gridlines.

To set the grid, do this:

1. Click Tools menu and choose Options... . The Options dialog box appears as shown in Figure 2.22.

2. Enable the Show grid check box, and enable one of the following options:

   - As lines
   - As dots

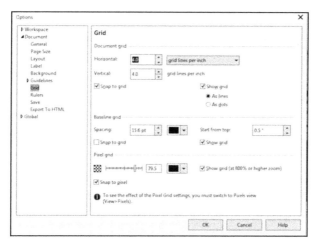

Figure 2.22 To set grid options in the Options dialog box

3. To display the grid as lines, click the **Show gird As** l̲ines radio button.

4. To display the grid as dots, click the Show gird **As** d̲ots radio button.

5. In the **Document grid** area, type a value in the

   Horizontal: list box type the distance between horizontal grid.

   Vertical: list box type the distance between vertical grid.

   If you want to change the grid spacing intervals or the number of lines displayed per unit of measure, choose an option from the list box. The options are based on the unit of measure used for the ruler

6. In the **Baseline grid** area, type a value in the **Spacing**: box to set spacing.

7. Type a value in the **Start from top**: box, to set distance from top. Setting this value to 0 makes the first line of the baseline grid overlap with the top edge of the drawing page.

8. To set color, open the **Color** picker, and choose a color and click OK button.

Snap to Grid

You can also make objects snap to gridlines so that when they are moved they jump between the nearest grid line or dot.

To get objects snap to grid do this:

1. Select the object that you want to snap to the target object.

2. Move the pointer over the object until the snap point becomes highlighted.

3. Drag the object close to the target object until the snap point on the target object becomes highlighted.

4. Click **Tools** menu and choose **Options**... or press **Ctrl+J** keys together.

5. In the **Document gird** area, click the check box **Snap to grid** as shown in Figure 2.22.

Spirals and Graphs

With CorelDRAW X8 you can draw spiral shapes and graphs. Symmetrical spirals expand evenly so that the distance between each revolution is equal. Logarithmic spirals expand with increasingly larger distances between revolutions. You can set the rate by which a logarithmic spiral expands outward.

Spirals

To draw spirals, do this:

1. Click the **Object** flyout and choose **Spiral** tool.

2. Specify the number of revolutions you want in the **Spiral Revolutions** list box.

3. Click and drag in the drawing window till the spiral is of the desired size (See Figure 2.23).

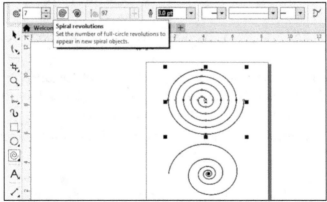

Figure 2.23 A symmetrical (above) logarithmic (below) spirals

4. If you do not want the spiral to be symmetrical, click on the Logarithmic Spiral button in the property bar.

5. Set the **spiral expansion factor** by dragging the slider on the property bar.

Note: You can draw a spiral from its center outward by holding down **Shift** *key as you drag. You can also draw a spiral with even horizontal and vertical dimensions by holding down* **Ctrl** *key as you drag.*

Graphs

To draw graph, do this:

1. Click the **Object** flyout and choose **Graph Paper** tool.

2. Click and drag in the drawing window till the graph is of the desired size is formed. (See Figure 2.24)

3. You can set the number of rows and columns in the Graph Paper Rows and Columns list box in the property bar. The top box specifies the number of columns and the bottom box specifies the number of rows.

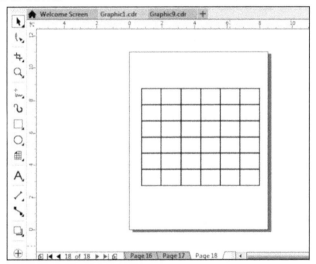

Figure 2.24 A graph with 6 rows and 6 columns drawn using the Graph Paper tool

Drawing by using shape recognition

You can use the Smart drawing tool to draw freehand strokes that can be recognized and converted to basic shapes.

You can set the amount of time to elapse between making a pen stroke and the implementation of shape recognition. For example, if the timer is set to one second and you draw a circle, shape recognition takes effect one second after you draw the circle.

To draw a shape by using shape recognition, do this:

1. In the toolbox, click the **Smart drawing** tool.

2. Set the level for detecting shapes and converting them to object by choosing a recognition level from the **Shape recognition level** list box on the property bar.

3. Choose a smoothing level from the **Smart smoothing level** list box on the property bar.

4. Set the level of smoothing the outline of shapes that are created with the Smart Drawing tool in the **Smart Smoothing Level** list box on the property bar.

5. Draw a shape in the drawing window as shown in Figure 2.25.

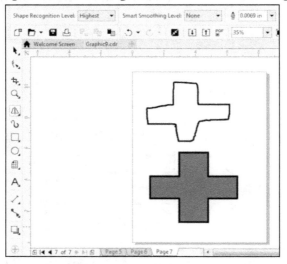

Figure 2.25 Using Smart Drawing tool to draw a shape

To set shape recognition delay

1. Click the Tools menu and choose Options... .

2. In the Workspace list of categories, click Toolbox, and then click Smart Drawing tool.

3. Move the Drawing assistance delay slider.

CHAPTER 3

Artistic Media Tool

Introduction

The Artistic media tool is used to draw curves like the Freehand tool. As in Freehand tool, Artistic media tool also draws a curve by clicking and then dragging.

Artistic Media tool is actually a collection of many tools. Each tool has its own settings and effects. When you click on the Artistic media tool in the Curve flyout, the property bar displays these different tools. When you click on a tool, the corresponding settings and effects are displayed on the property bar (See Figure 3.1).

Using Preset Tool

Preset line is the name given to thick lines that can be drawn in CorelDRAW X8 using the preset button. These lines can be drawn of different shapes according to the requirement.

CorelDRAW provides you certain preset lines that can be chosen to draw lines of your choice.

To draw a line using preset tool, do this:

1. Click the **Artistic media** tool in the toolbox.
2. Click the **Preset** button on the Property bar.
3. Choose a preset line shape from the **Preset stroke** list box. (See Figure 3.1) It shows the property bar displayed when Preset button is clicked. Click on the **Preset** drop down menu and choose a preset line.
4. If you want to smoothen the edges of the line, type a value in the **Freehand Smoothing** box on the property bar.

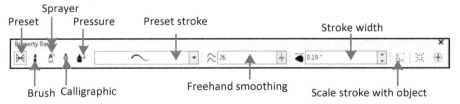

Figure 3.1 Property Bar for Artistic Media Preset Tool.

5. If you want to set the width of the line, type a value in the **Stroke width** box on the property bar.

6. Drag on the Drawing window with a mouse to shape the lines you want. You can apply fills also to these preset lines (See Figure 3.2).

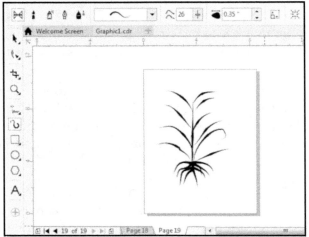

Figure 3.2   Using Preset tool to draw a grass

Using Brush Tool

With CorelDRAW X8, you can apply a variety of preset brush strokes. The width and smoothness of the brushstroke can be set according to your choice. The Brush Stroke List drop down menu lets you choose brush strokes ranging from strokes with arrow heads to one filled with rainbow patterns.

Note: You can also create custom brush strokes using an object or a group of vector objects. When you create a custom brush stroke, you can save it as a preset.

To apply brush stroke, do this:

1. Click the **Artistic media** tool on the Property bar.

2. Click on the **Brush** button in the Property bar. Figure 3.3 shows the Brush Stroke Property bar.

3. Choose the category for the selected Artistic media tool.

4. Choose a brushstroke from the **Brushstroke** list box.

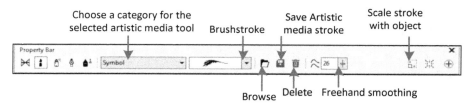

Figure 3.3   Artistic Media Brush Property Bar.

5. To smoothen the edges of the stroke, type a value in the **Freehand smoothing** box on the property bar.

6. To set the width, type a value in the **Stroke width** spinner box on the Property bar.

7. Drag on the Drawing window to shape your stroke (See Figure 3.4).

Figure 3.4   Different types of Brush Strokes

Note: If a brush stroke is not listed in the **Brush stroke** *list box, you can locate the brush stroke file by clicking the* **Browse** *button on the property bar.*

Using Object Sprayer Tool

The Object **Sprayer** tool provides effects that look nothing at all like the line you will draw.

To apply Sprayer tool effects, do this:

1. Click the Artistic media tool on the Property bar.

2. Click on the Sprayer button in the Property bar. Figure 3.5 shows the Object Spray Property bar.

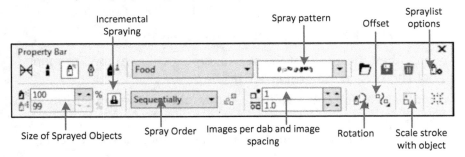

Figure 3.5   The Object Spray Property Bar

3. Choose a spray pattern category from the **Category** list box on the property bar

4. Drag and draw a line or curve. When you release the mouse button, you will see the selected spraylist applied (See Figure 3.6).

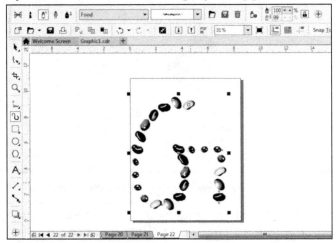

Figure 3.6   The category Food strokes of Spray pattern are drawn

5. Type a number in the bottom box of the Size of sprayed objects box on the property bar to increase or decrease the size of the spray objects as they progress along the line.

6. To set the spray order, choose a spray order from the **spray order** list box.

7. In the top box of the **Dabs/Spacing of objects to be sprayed** box, type a value, to adjust the number of objects sprayed at each point. Type a value in the bottom box to set the spacing between dabs.

8. Click the **Scale stroke with object** button on the property bar to apply transformations to spray line thickness when scaling.

9. Click the **Rotation** button, to rotate a line. In the **Angle** box, type a value for rotation.

   Enable the **Use Increment** check box to rotate each object in the spray and type a value for increment in the **Increment** box, to rotate step by step.

   Click the **Path based** radio button, to rotate objects in relation to line.

   Click the **Page based** radio button and Press Enter key, to rotate objects in relation to page.

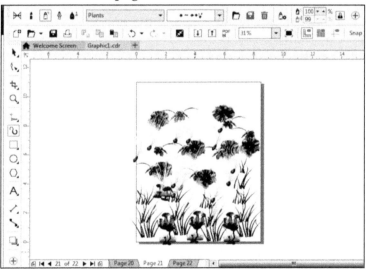

Figure 3.7   Using Sprayer tool a variety of spray pattern

10. Enable the **Use offset** check box to offset objects from the path of the line sprayed. If you want to adjust the offset distance, type a new value in the **Offset** box.

Using sprayer tool, you can create a variety of spray pattern as shown in Figure 3.7.

Using Calligraphic Tool

Calligraphic lines are similar to lines drawn using a calligraphic pen. Such lines change their thickness according to the direction of the line. Line's thickness also varies depending upon the angle of the pen nib.

To draw a Calligraphic line or curve, do this:

1. Click the **Artistic media** tool on the Property bar.

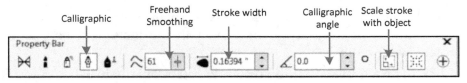

Figure 3.8 The Artistic Media Calligraphic Property Bar

2. Click the **Calligraphic** button on the Property bar. Figure 3.8 shows the Property bar for calligraphic button.

3. If you want to smoothen the edges of the line, type a value in the **Freehand Smoothing** box on the Property bar. If Property bar is not visible, right click the tool in the toolbox, and check Property bar.

4. Type a value in the **Calligraphic angle** box on the Property bar.

5. To set the width of the line, type a value in the **Stroke width** box on the property bar.

6. Apply transformations to line thickness when scaling, click the **Scale stroke with object** button on the property bar.

7. Drag until the line is the shape you want as shown in Figure 3.9.

Pressure Sensitive Lines or Curves

Pressure sensitive lines are those lines with curved edges that vary in width or thickness along a path. This effect can be created using mouse or a pressure sensitive pen.

To draw a pressure sensitive line or curve, do this:

1. Click the **Artistic media** tool on the property bar.

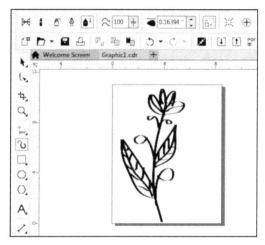

Figure 3.9 A flower drawn by using calligraphic pen stroke

2. Click the **Pressure** button on the Property bar. Figure 3.10 shows the property bar for the pressure sensitive line.

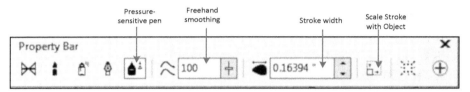

Figure 3.10 The Artistic Media Pressure Sensitive Pen Property Bar

3. To smooth the edges of the line, type a value or drag the slider in the **Freehand smoothing** box on the Property bar.

4. To change the width of the line, type a value in the **Stroke width** box on the Property bar.

5. Drag until the line is of the shape you want. Figure 3.11 shows a pressure-sensitive line.

Applying Artistic Media Effects

Till now, you were selecting the Artistic media effects that you needed from the Property bar. After selecting the desired effect you would drag and draw a curve in the drawing window. The selected effect gets applied to the curve. But by using the **Artistic media** docker window, you can apply changes to a curve, interactively. You can apply the desired artistic effect to an already drawn simple curve.

You can also replace an artistic media effect with another effect, which is not possible with property bar.

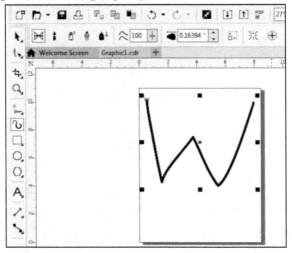

Figure 3.11 Drawing a Pressure Sensitive Curve

To use Artistic Media docker window, do this:

1. Draw any curve.

2. Click on the **Window** menu, highlight **Dockers**. A sub menu appears choose **Artistic Media**.

3. The top part of the Docker window shows the list of Artistic media tools you recently used. The bottom part of the window shows the effects (See Figure 3.12).

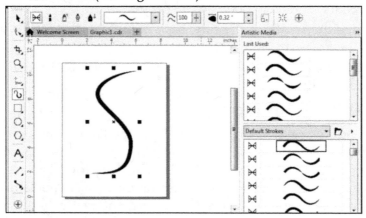

Figure 3.12 Artistic Media Docker Window

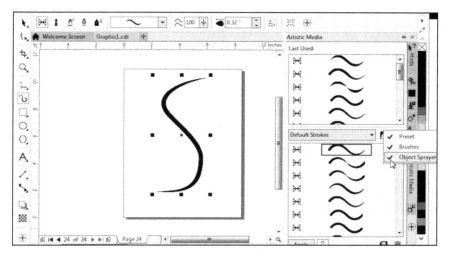

Figure 3.13 Choosing Type of Effect from the Docker Window

4. Click on the small triangle at the top right corner of the bottom window. In the menu that appears, select the type of effects you want. (See Figure 3.13)

5. Choose an effect from the Docker window. (See Figure 3.14)

6. Click Apply.

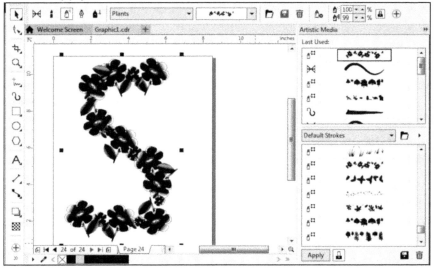

Figure 3.14 Clicking the brush stroke type from the styles

CHAPTER 4

Advanced Drawing

Introduction

In Chapter 3, you learnt to work with the basic tools and shapes available with CorelDRAW X8. In this Chapter, you will learn advance concepts used in drawings and managing the drawing objects using technique of grouping and ungrouping.

Grouping and Ungrouping Objects

A group is the name given to a set of objects that behave as a single unit on selection. Operations performed on a group of objects are applied equally to all the objects. A nested group is a group of two or more groups that behave as a single object.

Note: Once objects are grouped, you cannot work on individual objects. To work on an object individually, you will need to ungroup them.

To create a group of objects, do this:

1. Select the objects that you want to include in a group. To select all objects, click **E**dit menu and choose **Select A**ll and then **O**bjects. To select particular objects, select each object while holding the **Shift** key.

2. Click **Obj**ect menu highlight **G**roup and choose **G**roup Objects. Alternatively, press **Ctrl+G** keys together. Figure 4.1 shows grouped objects. The status bar indicates that a group of objects is selected.

To ungroup the grouped objects do this:

1. Select the group of objects you want to ungroup.

2. Click **Obj**ect menu highlight **G**roup and click one of the following commands:

   Ungroup objects — It breaks a group into individual objects, or a nested group into multiple groups.

   Ungroup all objects — It breaks one or more groups into individual objects, including objects within nested groups.

You can also ungroup objects by clicking the **Ungroup** button on the property bar.

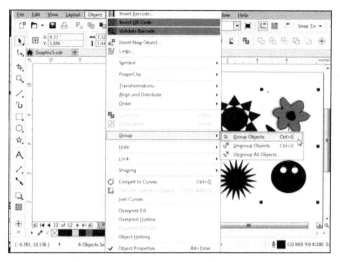

Figure 4.1   Grouping the objects

Note: You can also select one or more objects by dragging around the object.

Combining objects

Combining two or more objects creates a single object with common fill and outline attributes. You can combine rectangles, ellipses, polygons, stars, spirals, graphs, or text and they have converted in to a single curve object. If you need to modify the attributes of an object that has been combined from separate objects, you can break apart the combined object. You can extract a subpath from a combined object to create two separate objects. You can also weld two or more objects to create a single object.

To combine objects, do this:

1. Select the objects to be combined as shown in Figure 4.2.
2. Click **Object** menu and choose **C**ombine. Alternatively, press Ctrl+L keys together.

You can also combine selected objects by clicking the **Combine** button ▮ on the property bar.

To break apart a combined object, do this:

1. Select a combined object as shown in Figure 4.3.
2. Click **Object** menu and choose **C**ombine. Alternatively, press Ctrl+K keys together. The combined object get separated.

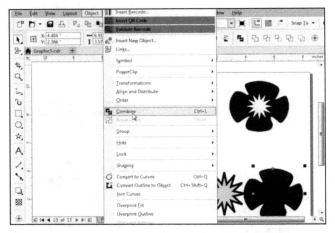

Figure 4.2   The two objects are combined to create a single object

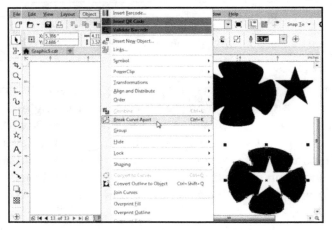

Figure 4.3   The selected objects break Curve Apart

To extract a subpath from a combined object, do this:

1. Click the **Shape** tool, and select a segment, node or group of nodes on a combined object as shown in Figure 4.4.

2. Click the **Extract subpath** button on the property bar.

After you extract the subpath, the fill and outline properties of the path have removed from the combined object.

In the following section you will learn to use the various editing tools in CorelDRAW X8. These tools are located in the **Shape Edit** flyout (See Figure 4.5) and their usage is discussed in the following sections.

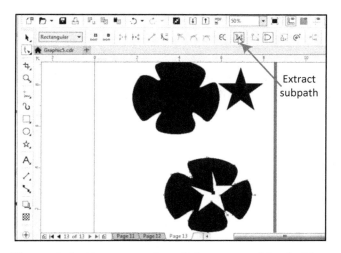

Figure 4.4 Extract a subpath from a combined object

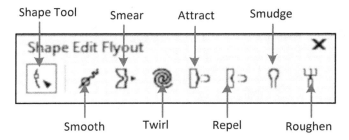

Figure 4.5 The Shape Edit flyout

Aligning and Distributing Objects

CorelDRAW X8 lets you align and distribute objects in a drawing. You can align objects with each other and with parts of the drawing page such as, center, edges. And you can align multiple objects with the centre of the drawing page horizontally or vertically. Single or multiple objects arranged along the edge of the page.

Distributing objects automatically adds spacing between objects, on their width, height and centre points. You can distribute objects so that their center points or selected edges (for example, top or right) appear at equal intervals. You can also distribute objects so that there is eqaul space between them. You can distribute objects over the extent of the boundary box surrounding them or over the entire drawing page.

To align an object with an object, do this:

1. Select the object with a pick tool.

2. Click Object menu choose Align and Distribute. The sub menu options appears, click the selected options you want to apply. Or click the Window menu highlight Dockers and then choose Align and Distribute. The Align and Distribute dockers window opens appears with objects shows left, center horizontally and right as shown in Figure 4.6.

3. Click the Align tab.

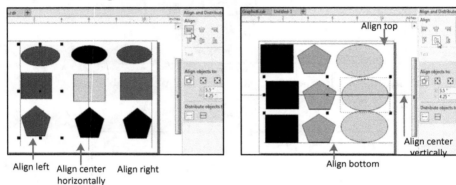

Figure 4.6   Align and Distribute window showing Align tab

4. Choose the desired options you want to specify horizontal and vertical alignment options.

   Align left — to align the left edges of objects.

   Align center horizontally — to align object centers along a vertical axis.

   Align center vertically —

   Align right — to align the right edges of objects.

   Align top — to align the top edges of objects.

   Align center vertically — to align object centers along a horizontal axis.

   Align bottom — to align the bottom edges of objects.

5. In the Align objects to area and choose the desired object from the list.

   Active objects button: Align an object with a specific object.

Page edge button: Align an object with the page edge.

Page center button: Align an object with the page center. To align the center of the object with the page center, make sure that the **Align center horizontally and vertically** button in the **Align** area are enabled.

Grid button: Align an object with the closest grid line.

Specified point button: Align an object with a specified point and type values in the Specify coordinates boxes.

6. If you are aligning text objects, choose one of the following options and shown in Figure 4.7.

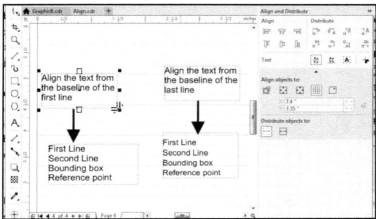

Figure 4.7   Align text from the baseline of the first line and last line

First line baseline — This uses the baseline of the first line of text as a reference point.

Last line baseline — This uses the baseline of the last line of text as reference point.

Bounding box — This uses the bounding box of a text object as reference point.

To Align an Object with a Specified Point do this:

1. Select the object with a pick tool. Or

2. If you want to align multiple objects, marquee select the objects.

3. Click Object menu choose Align and Distribute. A sub menu appears, and then click one of the following objects.

   Center to Page — It aligns all objects with the page center.

Center to page <u>V</u>ertically—It aligns objects with the page center along a vertical axis.

Center to page <u>H</u>orizontally—It aligns objects with the page center along a horizontal axis.

To distribute objects, do this:

1. Select the objects with the Pick tool.
2. In the Align and Distribute docker window click Distribute tab as shown in Figure 4.8.

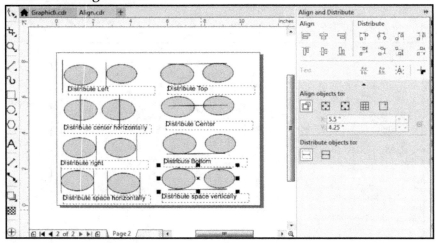

Figure 4.8   Showing Objects placed distribute horizontally and vertically

3. To distribute the objects horizontally, choose one of the following options from the top-right row:

   Distribute Left — It spaces objects' left edges.

   Distribute Center horizontally—It spaces the objects' center points along a horizontal axis.

   Distribute Spacing horizontally —It places equal intervals between the selected objects.

   Distribute Right — It spaces objects' right edges.

4. To distribute the objects vertically, choose one of the followin g options from the column on the left:

   Distribute Top — It evenly spaces the objects' top edges.

   Distribute Center Vertically — It evenly spaces the objects' center points.

Distribute Spacing Vertically — It places equal intervals between the selected objects.

Distribute Bottom — It evenly spaces the objects' bottom edges.

5. To indicate the area over which the objects are distributed, choose one of the following options:

    Extent of selection — It distributes the objects over the area of the bounding box surrounding them.

    Extent of page — It distributes the objects over the drawing page.

Order of Objects

You can change the stacking order of objects on a layer or a page by sending objects to the front or back, or behind or in front, of other objects. You can also position objects precisely in the stacking order, as well as reverse the stacking order of multiple objects.

To change the order of an object, do this:

1. Select the object with the Pick tool.

2. Click **Object** menu and choose **Order**, a sub menu appears and choose the one of the following options. (See Figure 4.9)

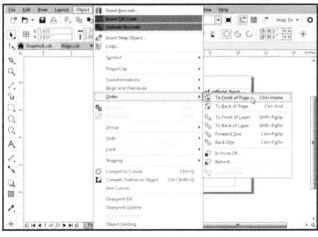

Figure 4.9   Selecting the stacking order of an objects

To Front of Page — The selected object moves in front of all other objects on the page.

To Back of Page — The selected object moves behind all other objects on the page.

To Front of Layer — The selected object moves in front of all other objects on the active layer

To Back of Layer — The selected object moves behind all other objects on the active layer

Forward One — The selected object moves forward one position. If the selected object is in front of all other objects on the active layer, it is moved to the layer above.

Back One — The selected object moves behind one position. If the selected object is behind all other objects on the selected layer, it is moved to the layer below.

In front of — The selected object moves in front of the object that you click in the drawing window.

Behind... — The selected object moves behind the object that you click in the drawing window.

Figure 4.10 shows different types of stacking order of objects.

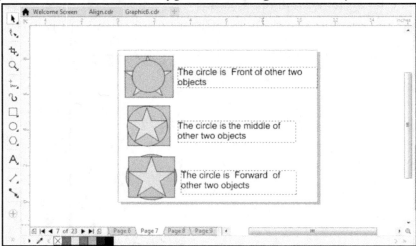

Figure 4.10 Different types of stacking order of an objects

To arrange in reverse order, do this:

1. Select multiple objects with the **Pick tool**, either by clicking individually with **Shift** key pressed, or by marquee selection.

2. Click **Object** menu, highlight **Order** and choose **Reverse Order**. The objects are rearranged in reverse order.

*Note: An **Order** command is unavailable if the selected object is already positioned in the specified stacking order.*

Using Nodes Types

You can change the nodes on a curve object to one of four types: cusp, smooth, symmetrical, or line (See Figure 4.11). The control handles of each node type behave differently.

Cusp nodes let you create sharp transitions, such as corners or sharp angles, in a curve object. Smooth nodes, the lines passing through the node take on the shape of a curve, producing smooth transitions between line segments. With smooth nodes, the lines passing through the node take on the shape of a curve, producing smooth transitions between line segments. Line nodes let you shape curve objects by changing the shape of their segments. You can make a curved segment straight or a straight segment curved.

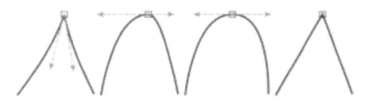

Figure 4.11 Different Nodes types

To manipulate the segments of a curve object, do this:

1. In the toolbox, click the **Shape** tool.
2. Click a curve object.
3. Perform a task from the following options are:

   - **Straighten a curve segment:** Click a curve segment, and click the **Convert to line** button ⟋ on the property bar.

   - Curve a straight segment: Click a straight segment, and click the **Convert to curve** ⟿ button on the property bar.

   - **Smooth a segment:** Click a node, and move the **Curve smoothness** slider on the property bar. To smooth all segments in a curve object, select all of the object's nodes before moving the **Curve smoothness** slider.

   - Change the direction of a curve object: Click a segment, and click the **Reverse direction** button ⫯ on the property bar.

Editing Curves with Nodes

The small square points at the end of a line or a curve segment are called nodes. These nodes can be dragged or pulled anywhere to change the shape of a line, curve or other shapes.

To select or deselect node(s) from the object, do this:

1. Click the Shape edit flyout, and choose the Shape tool in the Toolbox.
2. Select the object for which you want to edit the nodes.
3. Click a node on the curve object i.e. a small box in the object.
4. To select multiple nodes, hold down Ctrl key, and click each node.
5. To select all nodes, click the Edit menu, highlight Select All and choose Nodes.
6. To deselect a node hold down Ctrl key, and click a selected node.
7. To deselect multiple nodes, hold down Ctrl key, and click each selected node.
8. To select consecutive nodes, hold down Shift, click the first node, and then the last node that you want to select.
9. To select the first or last node of a curve object, press Home or End key.
10. To select the node that follows or precedes a selected node, press Tab or Shift + Tab.

To add a node, do this:

1. Click the Shape edit flyout and choose the Shape tool.
2. Select the curve object, and double-click where you want to add a node as shown in Figure 4.12, or **Add nodes** on the property bar.

To delete a node, do this:

1. Click the Shape edit flyout and choose the Shape tool.
2. Select the curve object, and double-click the node, which you want to delete.

To rotate and skew nodes, do this:

1. Click the Shape edit flyout and choose the Shape tool.
2. Select a curve object.
3. Select the nodes along the curve, which you want to transform.

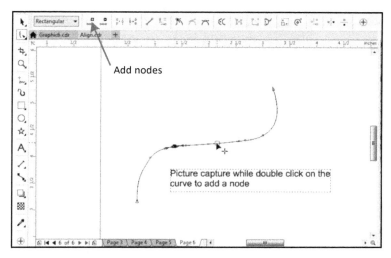

Figure 4.12 Adding nodes

4. From the Property bar, choose **Stretch or scale nodes** or **Rotate and skew nodes** (See Figure 4.13).

5. Drag a set of handles to transform the nodes.

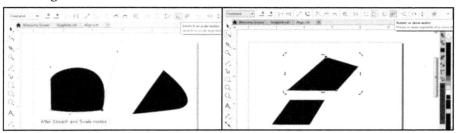

Figure 4.13 Drag the nodes to Stretch and Scale (Left) and Rotating nodes (Right) the object

Editing Shapes using Nodes

Like curves we can also edit other shapes such as *ellipses, rectangles* or *polygons.*

To edit shapes do this:

1. Click the **Shape edit** flyout and choose the **Shape** tool.

2. Click the shape you want to edit with this tool.

3. Nodes will appear (See Figure 4.14). Move these nodes to change the shape of the rectangle, polygon or ellipse.

- Edges of rectangle become rounded when one of the nodes along the outline of the rectangle is dragged.
- Square can be converted into a circle with the help of nodes. Drag any of the four nodes situated at the corners. Drag the node to the Rounded rectangle edges and the square will be converted into a circle. (See Figure 4.14)
- Polygons can be converted into stars by dragging on the side or corner nodes (See Figure 4.15). And a star can be converted into a fan like figure. (See Figure 4.16)

4. Ellipses and circles have only a single node. This node can be dragged with the Shape tool to create an arc or pie (See Figure 4.17).

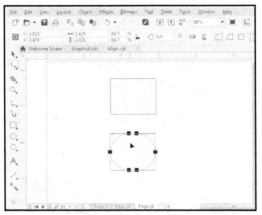

Figure 4.14 Square being converted into a circle

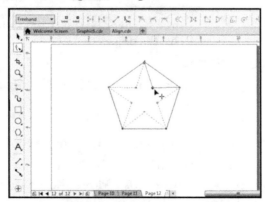

Figure 4.15 Polygon being converted into a star by dragging node

Note: When you click and drag any of the nodes on a shape, the effect is applied to all the nodes. If you wish to work on individual nodes you will have to convert the shape into curve.

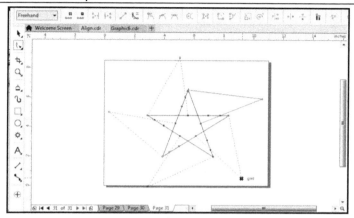

Figure 4.16 5-point star being converted using shape tool

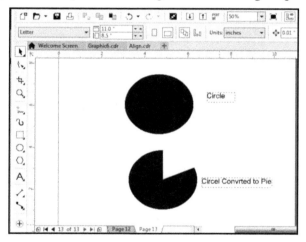

Figure 4.17 By dragging the node, the circle is made into pie-slice shape

To edit individual nodes, do this:

1. Select the shape.
2. Click **Object** menu and choose **Convert to curves**.
3. *Alternatively*, you can click on the **Convert To curve** button on the property bar.

You can now drag and modify each node as you like.

Smoothing Objects

You can smooth curved objects to remove jagged edges and reduce the number of nodes. You can control the size of the brush nib and the speed at which the effect is applied and the smoothing effect.

To smooth an object, do this:

1. Select the object with the pick tool.

2. Click the **Smooth** tool on the toolbox.

3. Drag along the edge of the object.

4. Type a value in the **Nib size** box on the property bar to set the size of the brush nib.

5. Type a value in the **Rate** box to set the speed of the smoothing effect.

6. Use the pressure of a digital pen to control the effect **Pen pressure** button on the property bar. You can see the smooth effect of text as shown in Figure 4.18.

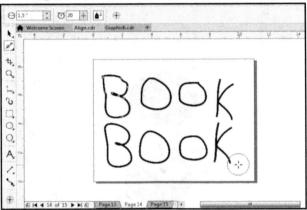

Figure 4.18 Text converted to curves (top) and the same text smoothed with the **Smooth** tool (bottom)

To smear an object, do this:

1. Select the object on which you want to apply smear effect.

2. Click the **Smear** tool on the toolbox.

3. Do one of the following:

   • To smear the outside of an object, click outside an object, close to its edge, and drag outwards.

- To smear the inside of an object, click inside an object, close to its edge, and drag inwards.

4. To change the size of the brush nib type a value in the **Nib size** box on the property bar.

5. Set the amount of smearing, type a value in the **Pressure** box.

6. Click the **Pen pressure** button on the property bar to control the mount of smearing.

7. Click the **Smooth smear** button, to use smooth curves when smearing.

8. Click the **Pointy smear** button to use curves with sharp corners when smearing. You can see in Figure 4.19 to see the smear effect.

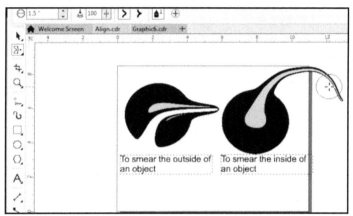

Figure 4.19 Showing smear outside and inside of an object

Using Smudge Brush Tool

Smudging means distort (alter or twist) an object by dragging the outline of the object or a group of objects. While applying smudging to an object, you can control the extent and shape of the distortion. The smudging effect depends on the angle of bearing and the tilt.

To smudge an object, do this:

1. Select the object on which you want to apply smudging effect.

2. Click the **Shape edit** flyout and choose the **Smudge Brush** tool.

3. Drag around the outline to distort it. (See Figure 4.20)

4. To change the size of the nib, type the value in the **Nib Size** box on the property bar.

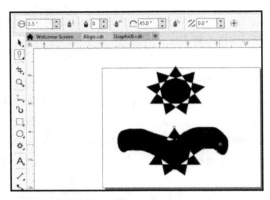

Figure 4.20 Smudging an object

5. Click the **Pen pressure** button on the property bar and apply pressure to the stylus.

6. To widen or narrow the smudging effect, type a value between -10 to 10 in Dry out box on the property bar.

7. Type a value between 15 and 90 in the **Tilt** box on the property bar.

8. To specify the shape of the smudging, type a value between 1 and 90 in the Pen tilt box on the property bar.

Note: To smudge the inside of an object, click outside of an object and drag inwards. To smudge the outside of an object, click inside of an object and drag outwards.

9. To specify the angle of the nib shape for smudging, type a value in the Pen bearing box on the property bar.

Shaping Objects by Attracting or Pushing away Nodes

The **Attract** and **Repel** tools let you shape objects by attracting nodes or pushing nodes away.

To shape an object by attracting or pushing nodes, do this:

1. Select the object on which you want to shape an object by attracting or pushing nodes.

2. In the toolbox, click the **Attract** tool.

3. Click inside or outside the object, close to its edge, and hold down the mouse button to reshape the edge.

4. Set the size of the brush nib, type a value in the **Nib size** box on the property bar.

To change the size of the brush nib, you can also drag in the document window while holding down **Shift** key. Drag towards the nib's center to decrease the radius, and away from the nib's center to increase it.

5. Set the speed of the attraction, type a value in the **Rate** box. Figure 4.21 shows the shape of arrow and start object by attracting and pushing the nodes.

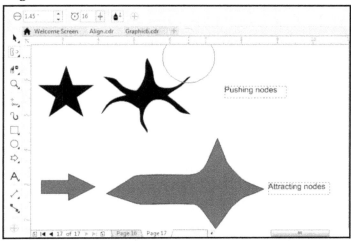

Figure 4.21 Showing Attracting and Pushing the nodes

Using Roughen Brush Tool

The Roughen Brush tool applies a jagged or spiked edge to objects, including lines, curves, and text. You can control the size, angle, direction, and number of the indentations.

To roughen an object, do this:

1. Select an object using the Pick tool.

2. Open the **Shape edit** flyout, and click the **Roughen** tool.

3. Point to the area on the outline you want to roughen, and drag the outline to distort it. (See Figure 4.22)

4. To specify the size of the roughening spikes, type a value in the **Nib size** box on the property bar.

   To change the number of spikes in a roughened area, type a value between 1 and 10 in the **Frequency of spikes** box on the property bar.

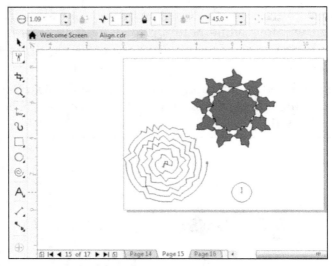

Figure 4.22 Applying roughen brush

5. To specify the height of the roughening spikes, Type a value between 1 and 90 in the Tilt box on the property bar.

6. To increase/decrease the number of roughening spikes, type a value between -10 and 10 in the Dry out box on the property bar.

7. To specify the direction of the roughening spikes Choose from the Fixed direction from the Spike direction list box. Type a value between 0 and 359 in the Bearing box on the property bar.

8. To create roughening spikes perpendicular to the path or outline, choose Auto from the Spike direction list box on the property bar.

Using Free Transform Tool

Using the free transform tool of the **Shape edit flyout,** you can transform the shape of any figure along a particular node.

To transform a drawing using free transform tool, do this:

1. Click on the Pick tool and choose the **Free Transform** tool.

2. To rotate the figure along a node choose **Free Rotation** button from the property bar. Then click on any node and drag to a point. You will see that the object pivots on that node (See Figure 4.23).

3. Type a value in the **Angle of rotation** box on the property bar.

4. **Free Angle Reflection** button creates a mirror image of the object in the angle you define (See Figure 4.24).

Figure 4.23 A Picture has been pivoted using the Free Rotation tool

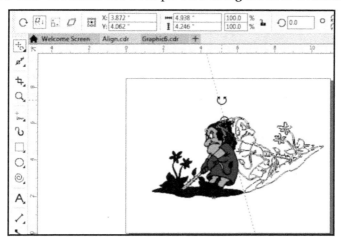

Figure 4.24 Picture of the woman has been mirror reflected using the Angle Reflection tool

5. The **Free Scaling** button on the property bar to be used to change the horizontal and vertical length of the object (See Figure 4.25).

6. Free **Skewing** button changes the shape of the object when a node is dragged (See Figure 4.26).

7. Type values in the **Skew angle** boxes on the property bar to specify the number of degrees by which you want to skew the object horizontally or vertically.

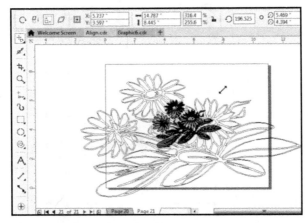

Figure 4.25 The image has been scaled to a larger size than its original size

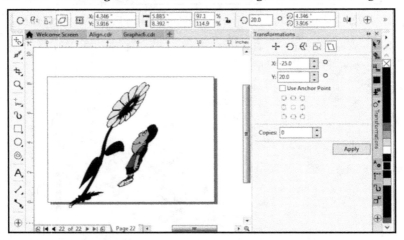

Figure 4.26 Image skewed using the Free Skew tool

Cropping objects

Cropping means remove unwanted areas of imported graphics objects in an image. When cropping objects, you define a rectangular area (cropping area) that you want to keep. Object portions outside the cropping area are removed. You can specify the exact position and size of the cropping area, and you can rotate and resize it. You can also remove the cropping area.

To crop objects, do this:

1. Select the object(s) that you want to crop using the Pick Tool.

2. Open the **Crop Tool** flyout, and click the **Crop Tool**. The cursor changes to crossangle.

3. Drag to define a cropping area as shown in Figure 4.27.

4. Double-click inside the cropping area. Only the cropped area remains.

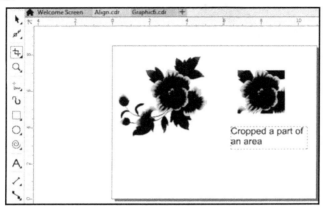

Figure 4.27 Cropping of image

Using Knife Tool

The knife tool as the name indicates cuts the object into pieces. You will now learn how to use this tool to cut drawings.

To edit drawing with knife tool, do this:

1. Click the **Crop** flyout and choose the **Knife** tool.

2. Click once on the outline of the figure where you want to break.

3. Then click at another point where you want to end the cut.

4. A line will be drawn between these two points.

5. Click the Pick tool and drag the two pieces apart from each other.

Figure 4.28 shows a triangle divided into a triangle and a trapezium using the knife tool.

Using Eraser Tool

Eraser tool is used to remove the unwanted parts or pixels of an object. Eraser tool is also used to draw white drawings on black background.

To erase a part of a drawing, do this:

1. Select the object on which you want to use the Eraser tool.

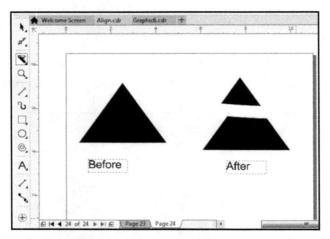

Figure 4.28 Triangle is divided into a trapezium with knife tool

2. Click the **Shape edit** flyout and choose the **Eraser** tool.
3. Drag over the object, which you do not want (See Figure 4.29).
4. To change the size of the eraser nib type a value in the **Nib size** box on the property bar, and press **Enter**.
5. To change the shape of the eraser nib, click the **Round nib** or the **Square nib** button on the property bar.
6. Disable the Reduce nodes button on the property bar, to maintain all the nodes of the area being erased.

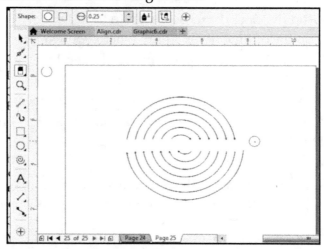

Figure 4.29 Spiral object being erased with the Eraser tool

Using Virtual Segment Delete Tool

With the help of Virtual Segment delete tool, you can delete portions of objects, (called virtual line segments) that are between intersections.

To delete a portion of the object or a ine segment, do this:

1. Open the Crop flyout, and click the Virtual Segment Delete tool.
2. Move the pointer to the line segment and then click the line segment. (See Figure 4.30)

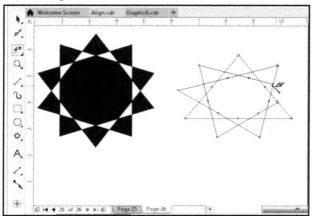

Figure 4.30 Virtual segment delete tool deletes the line segment

3. If you want to delete multiple line segments at one time, click the pointer to drag a marquee around all line segments you want to delete.

Note: The Virtual segment delete *tool sudden move upright when positioned properly and it does not work on linked groups.*

Drawing using Shape Recognition (Smart Drawing Tool)

CorelDRAW X8 provide you a facility to draw freehand strokes that are recognized and converted to basic shapes using the **Smart drawing** tool. It automatically smoothes any unrecognized shapes or curves drawn with the **Smart drawing** tool. If an object is not converted to a shape, it can be beautified. Objects and curves drawn with shape recognition are editable.

To draw a shape using smart drawing tool, do this:

1. Click the Smart drawing tool from the toolbox.

2. Choose a level of recognize an object from the **Shape Recognition level** list box on the property bar.

3. Choose a level of smoothing an object from the **Smart Smoothing level** list box on the property bar.

4. Draw a shape in the drawing window. (See Figure 4.31)

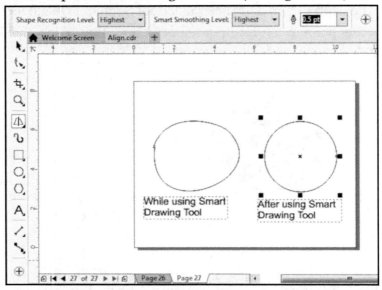

Figure 4.31 Draw an object using Smart Drawing tool

Filleting, Scalloping, and Chamfering Corners

You can shape an object by filleting, scalloping, or chamfering corners. (See Figure 4.32). Filleting produces a rounded corner, scalloping rounds and inverts the corner to create a notch, and chamfering bevels a corner so that it appears flat as seen in Figure 4.32.

You can fillet, scallop, or chamfer the corners of any curved object, whether it originates from a shape, lines, text, or a bitmap. If you select a shape that has not been converted to curves, a dialog box appears and gives you the option of converting the shape automatically. Text objects must be converted to curves manually by using the Convert to curves command. Changes apply to all corners unless you select individual nodes. You cannot fillet, scallop, or chamfer a smooth or symmetrical curve.

To apply filleting/scalloping/chamfering do this:

1. Select the object using the Pick Tool.

   Click <u>W</u>indows menu highlight <u>D</u>ockers and choose Fillet/Scallop/C<u>h</u>amfer to show the docker. Or Select the object with Pick tool and choose the Corner radius spinner box in the Property bar as shown in Figure 4.32.

2. In the docker window choose Fillet radio button list box.

3. Type a value in the **Radius:** list box.

4. Click **Apply.**

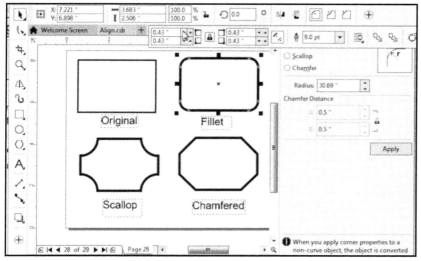

Figure 4.32 Filleting, scalloping and chamfering of objects

PowerClip Objects Creation

CorelDRAW X8 lets you place vector objects and bitmaps, such as photos, inside other objects, or containers. A container can be any object, for example artistic text or a rectangle. When you place an object into a container that is larger than the container, the object, called the content, is cropped to fit the form of the container. This creates a PowerClip object.

To show the effect of PowerClip command, objects of Flowerpot and Flower have shown in Figure 4.33. The picture in Figure 4.34 shows what happens when the flowerpot is the container and the flower is the content.

Figure 4.33 Showing Flowerpot and flower

To create a PowerClip object, do this:

1. Use the **Pick** Tool to select the objects that you want to use as the PowerClip contents.

2. Click **Object** menu, highlight **PowerClip** and choose **Place Inside Frame…** . The cursor changes to a big black arrow as shown in Figure 4.34.

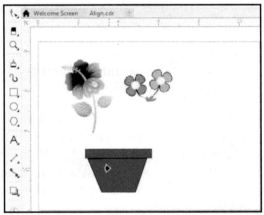

Figure 4.34 The Arrow head placed inside the container

Note: If you want to create a nested PowerClip, hold down the right mouse button, drag the PowerClip object inside a container, release the mouse button and click PowerClip Inside in the menu displayed.

3. Place the arrow inside the container and click. The selected contents are transferred, the Effect of PowerClip as shown in Figure 4.35.

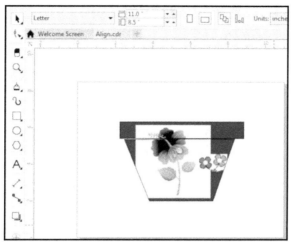

Figure 4.35 Effect of PowerClip the flowerpot is the container and flower is the content

To Extract Contents of a PowerClip Object, do this:

1. Select the PowerClip object.
2. Click **Objects** menu highlight **PowerClip** and choose **Extract Contents.**
3. The contents are separated.

To Edit Contents of a PowerClip object, do this:

After a PowerClip is created CorelDRAW allows you to edit the contents of the PowerClip without extracting the contents.

1. Select the PowerClip objects.
2. Click **Objects** menu highlight **PowerClip** and choose **Edit PowerClip Contents.**
3. Edit the contents of the PowerClip object.

   While you edit, the container appears in the Wireframe mode and cannot be selected.
4. When you finish editing click **Objects** menu highlight **PowerClip** and choose Finish Editing This Level.

CHAPTER 5

Working with Text

Creating Artistic Text in Paragraphs

CorelDRAW X8 enables string of text manipulated just as any other graphic objects. Two types of text you can add to drawings. These are:

- Artistic text and Paragraph text

Artistic texts are short lines of text to which you can apply a wide range of effects, such as drop shadows etc. Artistic text can be *sized, shaped, distorted, filled, outlined* and even converted to *curves.* (See Figure 5.1).

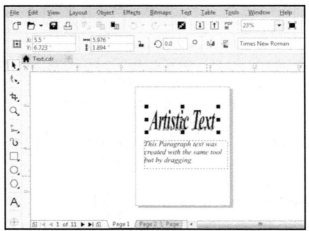

Figure 5.1 The Difference between Artistic and Paragraph Text

Paragraph texts are larger bodies of text that have greater formatting requirements. In fact, paragraph text is more like body text. It can be flowed, indented, hyphenated, put in column, etc. Paragraph text is better suited for editing long blocks of text as shown in Figure 5.1.

When to use Artistic Text?

Use artistic text in the following situations:

- **When you stretch and skew** — Artistic text can easily be scaled and stretched. Paragraph text can also be scaled, stretched or skewed with its frame by using the Alt key.

- **When you mirror, extrude, envelope, or change perspective**
These are the effects that can be applied to artistic text only. The Envelope effect can be applied to paragraph text, but when used with artistic text, envelope and other special effects actually bend characters.

- **For editing character shapes** — If you want to change the very shape of text characters by converting them to curves and then editing the nodes, you must use artistic text.

Note: Convert to curves command, does not work with paragraph text.

Working with Artistic Text

When you create artistic text, you make a graphic image that can be edited like any other graphic in CorelDRAW. You can easily resize or reshape artistic text, edit the graphical aspects, and also the text content and format.

Use artistic text for smaller blocks of text. Icons, Web sites banners, news-letters, master heads, and other text application with few characters.

Creating Artistic Text

To add artistic text, do this:

1. Click the Text tool in the toolbox.

2. Click anywhere in the drawing window using the Text tool and type any sentence. In Figure 5.1 the text written on top is an artistic text.

3. After you finish typing text, click on the Pick tool. When you click on the Pick tool, your text will be surrounded with eight small, square black handles as shown in Figure 5.2.

4. Click the Text menu and choose Con_v_ert To Artistic Text, or press Ctrl + F8 keys together. Artistic text appears in a bounding box in the document window as shown in Figure 5.2.

When to use Paragraph Text?

Use Paragraph text in the following situations:

- **To set large blocks of copy** — If artistic text is appropriate for the headline of an article, paragraph text is perfect for the article itself.

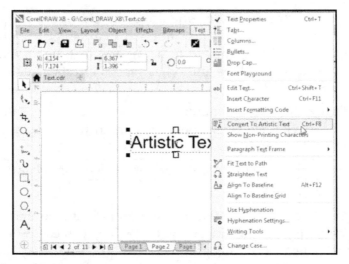

Figure 5.2 Select Convert To Artistic Text to add artistic text

Paragraph text can accommodate thousands of individual paragraphs, and thus, you can create many pages of text.

- **To control text flow** — Paragraph text can flow from frame to frame and from page to page. Also, you can easily change the length of the paragraph text.
- **To control the baselines of text** — A handy use for paragraph text is when you want to rotate the whole text along an angle.

Creating Paragraph Text

For creating paragraph text, you must create a text frame for each paragraph text object that you want to add.

To create paragraph text, do this:

1. Click the Text tool.
2. Drag the tool in the drawing window to size a paragraph text frame and then type inside the text frame. (See Figure 5.3)

Switching between Artistic and Paragraph text

If you create text in one form and discover that you really need it to be of other form, you can still convert text from one form to another form easily.

To switch between artistic and paragraph text, do this:

1. Click the Pick tool and right-click the text.

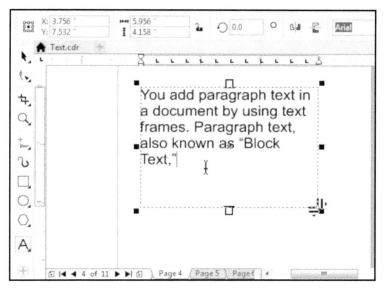

Figure 5.3 Paragraph Text frame showing entering text

2. If you want to convert Paragraph text to Artistic text choose **Convert To Artistic Text.**

3. If you want to convert Artistic text to Paragraph text, choose **Convert To Paragraph Text.**

To add text on an object, do this:

1. Using a drawing tool, draw a closed shape.

2. Create a text frame from an object by using the **Text** tool.

3. Move the cursor over the object's outline.

4. Click the object when the pointer changes to cursor as shown in the top ellipses as shown in Figure 5.4.

5. Type outside the frame.

To add text inside an object, do this:

1. Create a text frame from an object by using the **Text** tool.

2. Move the cursor over the object's outline.

3. Click the object when the cursor changes to the cursor as shown in Figure 5.5. Type inside the frame.

You can also separate a text frame from a container object. When you do so, the text frame retains the object's shape.

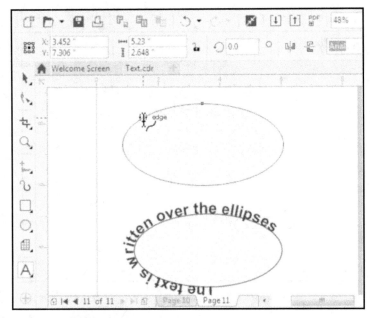

Figure 5.4 Writing text over an object

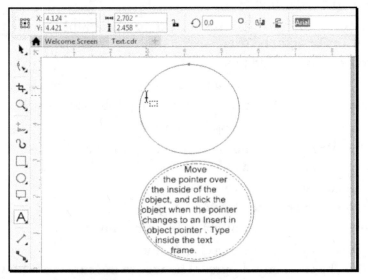

Figure 5.5 Writing a text inside the frame

To separate the text frame from an object, do this:

1. Select the object using the Pick tool.

2. Click Object menu and choose <u>B</u>reak Text Apart (if text written over an object) or choose <u>B</u>reak Paragraph Text inside a Path Apart (if text written inside an object).

3. Click a blank space in the drawing window and drag either the text frame or the object to a new location. In Figure 5.6, texts have been separated from the shapes (Inside and outside the frame).

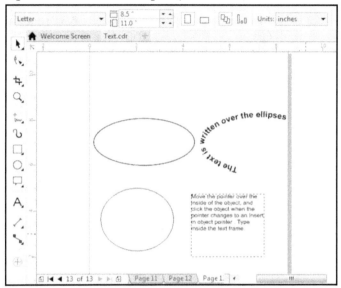

Figure 5.6 Text separated from the object

The Text Property Bar

The Text Property bar becomes active when you click the Text Tool. Text Property Bar is more useful for paragraph text than for artistic text. Table 5.1 explains the Text Property Bar tools and their uses.

As you see in Table 5.1, the Text Property Bar enables you to apply all types of formatting to the selected-text objects.

Table 5.1   Text Property Bar Tools

Tool	Name	What It Does?
Arial ▼	Font List	This drop down list enables you to select fonts to apply to the selected text.

(Contd...)

	Font Size List	Height from top of ascender to bottom of descender
18 pt ▼		
B	Bold	Assigns (or turns off) boldface for the selected text.
I	Italic	Assigns (or turns off) italic style for selected text.
U̲	Underline	Underlines the text in a selected text object.
	Horizontal Alignment	Align the block of text i.e. left, right, center, full justify and force full justify.
	Show/Hide Bullets	Inserts bullets on the left of text.
	Show/Hide Drop cap	Inserts drop cap at the beginning of a character.
A₀	Text	Opens Text properties
abl	Edit Text	Opens the Edit Text dialog box.

Formatting Text

The *Paragraph formatting* and *Character formatting* dockers give you easy access to commonly used text formatting options. In addition, the new commands on the Text menu let you easily add *tabs, columns, bullets,* and *drop caps* and insert formatting codes, such as em dashes and nonbreaking spaces.

Fonts vs. typefaces

"Font" and "typeface" are two typography terms that are often used interchangeably. A font is a collection of characters that includes letters, numbers, and symbols of one variation of a typeface, such as bold or italic. A typeface, which is also known as a font family, is made up of several fonts that share similar design characteristics.

Typefaces come in different shapes and sizes and have unique characteristics and expressive qualities.

There are a few basic tips for choosing the right typeface. These are:

- Choose a typeface that best suits the tone of your design.

- Choose a typeface that is appropriate for the final output of your design.

- Use less typefaces in your document. The general rule is not to exceed three or four typefaces in a document.

- Make sure the typeface characters are easy to read and recognize.

- Make sure the typeface of heading stands out and look good when displayed at larger sizes.

To select text for editing, do this:

1. To select an entire text object, click the object using the Pick tool.

2. To select specific characters of artistic or paragraph text for editing, drag across the text using the Text tool.

Character Formatting

To change the font, do this:

1. Using the Text tool to select the character or block of text you want to change.

2. Click Text menu and choose Text Formatting or press Ctrl+T keys together The Text Properties dockers window opens. Or click Window menu highlight Dockers and then choose Object Properties press Alt + Enter keys together.

3. It opens Text Formatting docker window opens as shown in Figure 5.7 appears.

4. In the Character area of the Object properties docker, perform one of the following options.

- Choose a font (typeface) from the Font: drop-down list.

- Choose a style from the Font Style: list to apply in your text. You can choose between *Normal, Normal-Italic, Bold* and *Bold-Italics*.

- Set the font Size by choosing a Size from the Size: list box.

5. In the Character Effects options choose the desired options you want to apply.

To underline, overline, or strikethrough text, do this:

1. To Underline selected character click the underline drop-down list. Move the cursor over the options you can see the effects of the underline options and choose the desired one. (See Figure 5.8)

Figure 5.7 Character formatting docker window

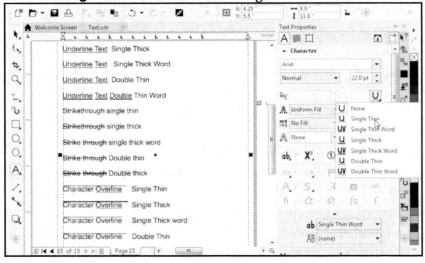

Figure 5.8 The Effects of underline, strikethrough and overline

2. To Strikethrough text, select the strikethrough option from the Strikethru: drop-down list (See Figure 5.8).

3. To Overline text, select the overline option from the Overline: drop-down list.

To change the text case, do this:

1. In the **Character** area of the **Object properties** docker, click the **Caps** button, and click one of the following options:

- **All Caps:** All the characters are in upper-case.

- **Titling Caps:** The first character of the first word is capitalized.

- **Small Caps:** All characters are in small font size and all small caps.

- **All Small Caps:** All character are in large font size and all uppercase

- **Small Caps from Caps:** All character are changed to lowercase letters.

2. Selected characters in the text can be positioned above or below the baseline. This can be printed by choosing *Superscript* or *Subscript* from the **Position**: drop-down list (See Figure 5.9).

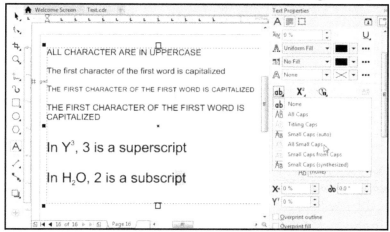

Figure 5.9 Text with different types of Caps and Subscript and superscript applied

3. *Alternatively*, after you select the text to which you want to apply formatting, select a new font and font size from the Property bar.

Note: Both Small caps and All caps will convert characters in your text to uppercase. But small caps will make the uppercase letters but smaller in height.

To resize text, do this:

1. Text can also be resized with the Pick tool, by clicking and dragging the corner selection handles. If you want to size paragraph text, you must press Alt key while you drag. Otherwise you size the frame that holds the text, not the text itself. (See Figure 5.10)

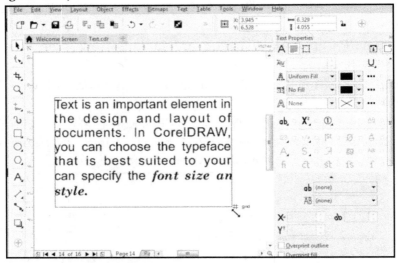

Figure 5.10 Paragraph text to be reized

Changing character position and angle

You can modify the appearance of text by shifting the characters vertically or horizontally, which changes the position of the selected characters relative to the surrounding characters. You can also rotate characters by specifying an angle of rotation.

To shift a character, do this:

1. In the **Character** area of the **Text Properties** docker, type a value in one of the following boxes:

   - **Angle** — Type the value in the Angle list box, a positive number rotates characters counter clockwise and a negative number rotates characters clockwise.

   - **Horizontal character offset** — Type the value in the horizontal shift list box, a positive number moves characters to the right, and a negative number moves characters to the left.

- **Vertical character offset** — Type the value in the vertical shift list box, a positive number moves characters up, and negative number character down.

To change the character position and angle are shown in Figure 5.11.

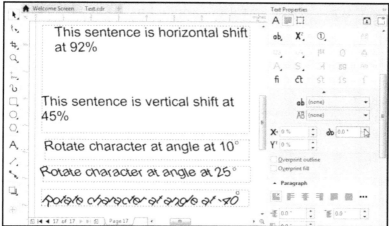

Figure 5.11   Different character position and angle

Paragraph Formatting

The Paragraph tab provides options for formatting the Paragraph.

To format paragraphs, do this:

1. Select the Paragraph text.

2. Click Te**x**t menu and choose Text **F**ormatting or press Ctrl+T keys together The Text Properties dockers window opens. Or click **W**indow menu highlight **D**ockers and then choose Object Properties press Alt + Enter keys together.

3. In the **Paragraph** area of the **Object properties** docker, click one of the following buttons:

- **No horizontal alignment** — It applies the default alignment setting.

- **Align left** — It aligns text with the left side of the text frame or the bounding box of artistic text.

- **Center** — It aligns text centers within the text frame.

- **Align right** — It aligns text with the right side of the text frame and the bounding box of artistic text.

- **Full justify** — It aligns text, with the exception of the last line, with the left and right sides of the text frame.
- **Force justify** — It aligns text, including the last line, with the left and right sides of the text frame.

Different types of alignment are applied in the text and shown in Figure 5.12.

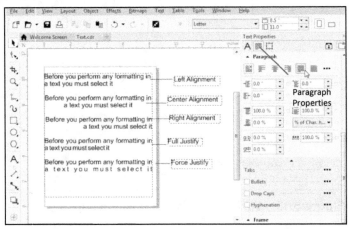

Figure 5.12 Different types of alignment

---

*Note: You can also align text horizontally by clicking the **Horizontal alignment** button on the property bar and choosing an alignment style from the list box.*

To align paragraph text vertically, do this:

1. In the **Object properties** docker, click the **Frame** button to display the frame-related options.

2. In the **Frame** area of the **Object properties** docker, choose an alignment option from the **Vertical** alignment list box as shown in Figure 5.13.

Adding Indents

Indenting changes the space between a text frame and the text that it contains. You can add and remove indents without deleting or retyping text. You can indent an entire paragraph, the first line of a paragraph, or all lines of a paragraph except the first line (a hanging indent). You can also indent from the right side of the text frame.

To indent paragraph text, do this:

1. In the Object properties docker, click the Paragraph button ▦ to display the paragraph-related options.

2. Specify indentations for your paragraphs from the Indents area.

   First line indent: In this list box, specify indents the first line of text relative to the left side of the frame.

   Left: In this list box, specify a hanging indent in which all but the first line of text is indented. (See Figure 5.14)

   Right: In this list box, specify indents for the right side of paragraph text.

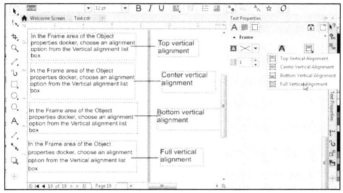

Figure 5.13 Different types vertical alignment options

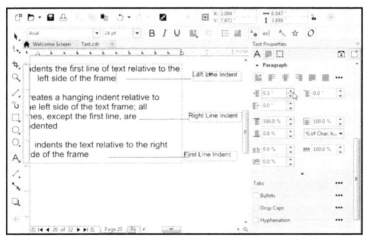

Figure 5.14 Different type of indentation

Adjusting line spacing and paragraph spacing

You can change the spacing between lines of text, which is also known as "leading" or "interline spacing." You can change the spacing between paragraphs. If a paragraph is positioned at the top or bottom of a frame, the spacing does not apply to the space between the paragraph text and the frame.

To adjust the spacing between paragraphs, do this:

1. In the Object properties docker, click the Paragraph button ☰ to display the paragraph-related options.

2. Adjust space between paragraph and lines within a paragraph from the **Spacing** area. You can also indicate spacing above and below paragraphs in a text frame (See Figure 5.15).

   Before paragraph: In this list box, you can specify the amount of space before the first line of a paragraph. And also you can choose the unit of measurement in which you want to specify the spacing between the lines.

   After paragraph: In this list box, you can specify the amount of space after the last line of a paragraph.

   Line spacing: In this list box, you can specify the amount of space between the text lines.

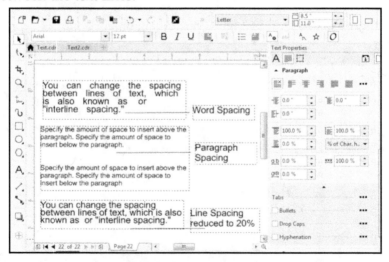

Figure 5.15 Adjust spacing between line, word and paragraph

Word Spacing: Specify the spacing between individual words in the Word Spacing list box.

The above line and word spacing options are shown in Figure 5.15.

Adding Tabs

Tab is used for setting the tab distance, tab alignment and trailing character.

1. In the Paragraph area of the Object properties docker, click the down arrow button located at the bottom of Paragraph area to display additional options.

2. Click the **Tab settings** button.

3. Click Te<u>x</u>t menu and choose Ta<u>b</u>s... .

4. Tab Settings dialog tab appears as shown in Figure 5.16.

Figure 5.16 Tab Settings dialog box

5. Click Tab location: list box, and then click Add button to specify the tab at which the tabs are to be set.

6. Click the cell in the Tabs column, specify the tab setting, the tab type, and whether the tab is selected.

7. Click the cell in the Alignment: column, specify the tab setting, the tab type, and whether the tab is lead.

8. Click the cell in the Leader... column, specify the tab setting, the tab type, and whether the tab is selected.

9. Click **Leader Options…** button. The **Leader Settings** dialog box appears as shown in Figure 5.17.

10. Choose the **Character**: list, specify the character for a leader tab for setting **Leader** options.

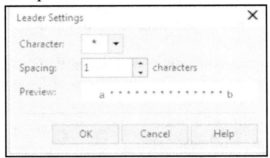

Figure 5.17 Leader Settings dialog box

11. Click **Spacing**: drop down list. You can change the spacing between characters in the trailing leader tab.

12. You can see the **Preview**: list box, whatever the changes you have applied.

13. If you want to Remove the selected tab setting click **Remove** button.

14. **Remove All** it means remove all tab settings.

15. Click OK. After applying the desired tab setting you can see the different tab setting as shown in Figure 5.18.

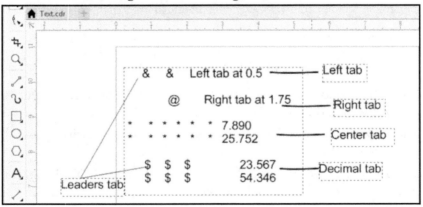

Figure 5.18 Different tab settings with Leader options

Setting Columns

The columns tab enables you to set text in columns. Columns are useful for designing text-intensive projects, such as newsletters, magazines, and newspapers. You can create columns of equal or varying widths and gutters.

To add columns to a text frame, do this:

1. Select the paragraph to be converted into columns.

2. In the **Object properties** docker, click the **Frame** button ⊓⊔ to display the frame-related options.

3. In the **Paragraph** area of the **Object properties** docker, click the down arrow button located at the bottom of **Paragraph** area to display additional options.

4. Click the **Columns** button in the Frame options. Type a value in the **Number of columns**: box.

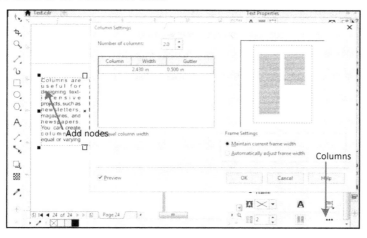

Figure 5.19   Column Settings dialog box

5. Or choose to click **T̲ext** menu and choose **C̲olumns**....

6. The **Column Settings** dialog box, appears as shown in Figure 5.19.

7. Type number of columns you want in the **Number of columns**: list box.

8. Specify column width and gutter. Gutter represents the spacing between each column.

9. If you want columns to be of equal width, click the **Equal column width:** check box.

10. Click **OK**. The selected no of columns appears in the drawing window as shown in Figure 5.19.

Using Bullets

Bullets are inserted at the beginning of each new line. You can use bulleted lists to format information. You can wrap text around bullets, or you can offset a bullet from text to create a hanging indent.

To use bullet, do this:

1. Select the paragraph to which you want to apply bullet.

2. In the **Paragraph** area of the **Object properties** docker, click the down arrow button located at the bottom of **Paragraph** area to display additional options.

3. Enable the **Bullets** check box.

4. Or click **T**ext menu and choose B**u**llets... .

5. Click the **Bullet settings** button ■■■, which is located to the right of the **Bullets** check box.

6. The **Bullets** dialog box appears as shown in Figure 5.20.

Figure 5.20   Bullets dialog box

7. In the **Appearance** area:

   Font: drop down list, choose a font for the bullet.

   Symbol: drop down list, and select desired symbol font.

Size: list box, specify the size of the bullet.

Baseline shift: specify the distance by which the bullet is offset from the baseline.

8. If you want to add a bullet with a hanging indent, enable the **use hanging indent style for bulleted list** check box.

9. In the **Spacing** area, type a value in the **Text frame to bullet**: box to specify the distance the bullet is indented from the paragraph text frame.

10. Type a value in the **Bullet to text**: box to specify the distance between the bullet and the text.

11. Click OK. The above bulleted option appears in the text frame as shown in Figure 5.21.

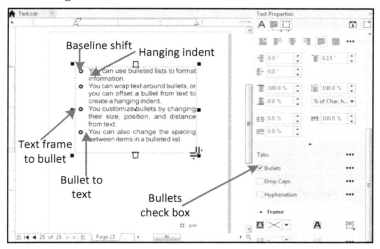

Figure 5.21 Setting bulleted options in the Text frame

Using Drop Cap

Applying drop caps, also known as initial caps, to paragraphs enlarges the initial letter and insets it into the body of text.

To add a Drop Cap, do this:

1. Click on **Text** tool and select the paragraph text to which you want to add a drop cap.

2. In the **Paragraph** area of the **Object properties** docker, click the down arrow button located at the bottom of **Paragraph** area to display additional options.

3. Enable the **Drop caps** check box.

4. Click the **Drop caps settings** button ▪▪▪. The **Drop Cap** dialog box appears as shown in Figure 5.22.

5. Or click **Text** menu and choose **Drop Cap...** . The **Drop Cap** dialog box appears.

Figure 5.22   Drop Cap dialog box

6. In the **Appearance** area, type the value in the **Number of line dropped:** list box.

7. Type a value in the **Space after drop cap:** box to specify the distance between the drop cap and the body of text.

8. Enable the **Use hanging style for drop cap** check box, if you want to have a hanging drop cap.

9. After applying setting, click OK.

Using Edit Text Feature

The Edit Text dialog box is very helpful, when you are editing large amount of text.

To use edit text, do this:

1. Select text object.

2. Click **Text** menu and choose the **Edit Text...** or press **Ctrl+Shift+T** The **Edit Text** dialog box appears as shown in Figure 5.23.

3. The **Edit Text** dialog box is a mini word processor in Windows. You can insert or delete text here. The **Edit Text** dialog box will even underline words not found in the dictionary with red line.

You can instantly look up correct spellings by right-clicking a word, as shown in Figure 5.23.

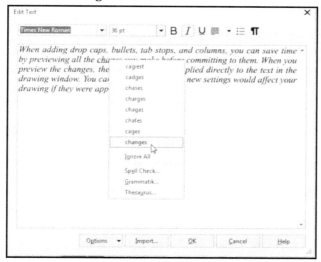

Figure 5.23 Edit Text dialog box

4. To add formatting, click on the Font attributes in the toolbar of Edit dialog box. Attributes assigned in this way will apply to the text.

5. When you have edited and assigned formatting to any text, click OK in the Edit Text dialog box.

6. The results will be visible in the CorelDRAW window.

Note: The Edit Text dialog box is not fully WYSIWYG (What You See Is What You Get). You have to click OK and view the results in the CorelDRAW window to see the exact effect of font attributes assigned to selected text.

Changing text color

You can quickly change both the fill and outline color of text. You can change the fill, outline, and background color of text. You can change the color of individual characters, a block of text, or all characters in a text object.

To quickly change the color of a text object, do this:

1. Using the **Pick** tool, click a text object to select it.

2. Perform a task from the following options:

3. To fill characters in a text object with one color, click any color swatch on the default color palette or drag a color swatch to the text object.

4. To apply an outline color to all characters in a text object, right-click any color swatch on the default color palette or drag a color swatch to the edge of a character in the text object

To change the color of a text selection, do this:

1. Using the **Text** tool, select a character or a block of text.

2. Click **W**indow menu highlight **D**ockers and choose **Object** proper**t**ies.

3. In the Object properties window, click the **Character** button to display the character-related options

4. In the **Character** area of the **Object properties** docker, perform one or more tasks from the following options.

- Choose the type of fill to apply the characters in the **Fill type** list box.

- Choose the Text color in the **Text color** list box as shown in Figure 5.24.

- To modify fill settings, click the **Fill settings** button ■ ■ ■, and modify the settings in the dialog box.

- In the text background color area, choose a fill type from the **Background fill type** list box, open the Fill picker, and then click a color or a fill.

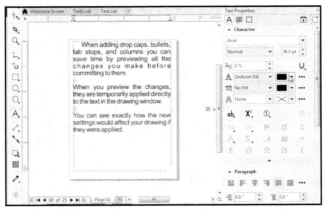

Figure 5.24 Selecting Text color in the Text properties docker window

Using Find and Replace

You can search text automatically using find and replace text facility in CorelDRAW. You can also find special characters, such as an em dash or optional hyphen. You can edit text directly in the drawing window or in a dialog box.

To search for a word in a block of text, do this:

1. Select the block of text.

2. Click Edit menu highlight Find and Replace and choose Find Text... . Alternatively, press Alt + F3 keys together. The Find Text dialog box appears as shown in Figure 5.25.

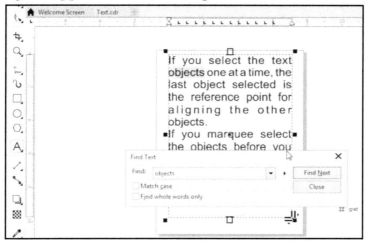

Figure 5.25 Find Text dialog box

3. Type the text you want to find in the Find: box.

4. Click Find Next button to begin the search again. After searching is completed, click Close button.

5. If you want to find the exact case of the text you specified, enable the Match case check box.

To find and replace text, do this:

1. Select the block of text.

2. Click Edit menu highlight Find and Replace and choose Find Text... . Alternatively, press Alt + F3 keys together. The Replace Text dialog box appears as shown in Figure 5.26.

3. Type the text that you want to find in the Find: box.

4. Type the replacement text in the **Replace With:** box.

5. Click one of the following buttons:

- **Find Next** — Finds the next occurrence of the text that is specified in the **Find** box.

- **Replace** — Replaces the selected occurrence of the text that is specified in the **Find** box. If no occurrence is selected, **Replace** finds the next occurrence.

- **Replace All** — Replaces every occurrence of the text that is specified in the **Find:** box.

6. For example here to change the word Objects instead of Object click Replace button to change the current occurrence of the word as shown in Figure 5.26.

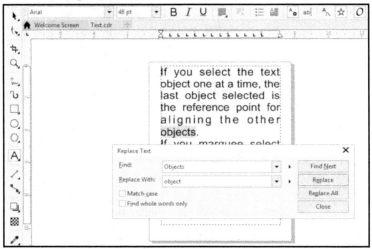

Figure 5.26 Replace Text dialog box

Using Spell Check

Spell check lets you check the text in several ways. You can use Spell check to check all of the spelling in a drawing, a portion of a drawing, or only selected text.

To Spell Check selected text, do this:

1. Select the text you want to check.

2. Click the **Text** menu, highlight **Writing Tools** and choose **Spell check... .**

3. The **Writing Tools** dialog box appears as shown in Figure 5.27. Click the **Spell Checker** tab. (This is selected by default).

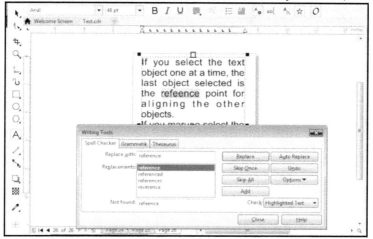

Figure 5.27 Writing Tools dialog box with Spell checker tab

4. Click <u>R</u>esume button to start.

5. In the **Replace <u>w</u>ith**: text box, choose the text that you want to replace the misspelled text.

6. In the **Rep<u>l</u>acements**: CorelDRAW displays the various options for the misspelled words text box, select a word and click the <u>R</u>eplace button.

7. Click the **Skip <u>O</u>nce** or **Skip <u>A</u>ll** button, to ignore the wrong word(s).

8. Click the **U<u>n</u>do** button to undo the spelling change.

9. After making changes, click <u>C</u>lose button.

Grammar checking text

Grammatik lets you check the text in this way. You can check the grammar in the selected text only.

To check Grammar, do this:

1. Select the sentence or paragraph for which the grammar needs to be checked.

2. Click the <u>T</u>ext menu and choose <u>W</u>riting Tools. In Writing Tools dialog box, click **Grammatik** tab property sheet as shown in Figure 5.28 appears.

3. Click **Start** button to begins a new check.

4. Click **Resume** button continues an interrupted check.

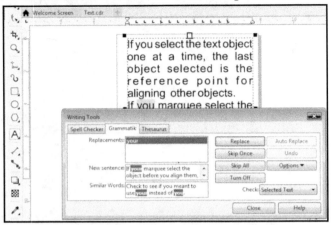

Figure 5.28   Grammatik tab in the Writing Tools dialog box

5. In the **Replacements**: text box, select the word or sentences, click the **Replace** button.

6. In the **New sentence**: list box, it displays a new sentence using the selected word in the **Replacements**: list box.

7. Any Grammatik words used in the sentence the words are highlighted in the **Similar words**: list box.

8. Click the **Skip Once** or **Skip All** button, to ignore the grammar mistake.

9. Click the **Undo** button to undo the spelling change.

10. After making changes, click the **Close** button.

Using Thesaurus

The Thesaurus lets you look up options such as Synonyms, Antonyms, and Related words, depending on the language and version of Thesaurus you are using.

To use Thesaurus, do this:

1. Select a word within a string or frame.

2. Click **Text** menu highlight **Writing Tools** and choose **Thesaurus**... . In **Writing Tools** dialog box, click **Thesaurus** tab as shown in Figure 5.29.

Figure 5.29 Thesaurus tab in the Writing Tools dialog box

3. It displays the selected word in the list box.

4. Click the Options button and choose Synonym. A list of synonym words appears in the bottom of the list box. Now you can select a word from the list.

5. If you choose Antonym, click the (plus sign), a list of opposite word appear, choose desired word.

6. Click the Replace button, to replace and insert words from the Thesaurus list box to where the cursor is placed in the document.

7. After making changes, click Close button.

Using QuickCorrect

QuickCorrect automatically corrects misspelled words and capitalization errors. You can customize QuickCorrect by specifying which types of errors you want to correct automatically.

To customize QuickCorrect, do this:

1. Click the Text menu highlight Writing Tools and choose QuickCorrect... .

2. Enable any of the following check boxes:

- Capitalize first letter of sentences.

- Correct two initial, consecutive capitals.

- Capitalize names of days
- Automatic hyperlink
- Replace text while typing

*The **Correct two initial, consecutive capitals** option doesn't make a change when a capital letter is followed by a space or period, or if a word contains other capital letters.*

To add words to QuickCorrect, do this:

1. Click the **Text** menu highlight **Writing Tools** and choose **QuickCorrect...** . The **Options** dialog box appears as shown in Figure 5.30.

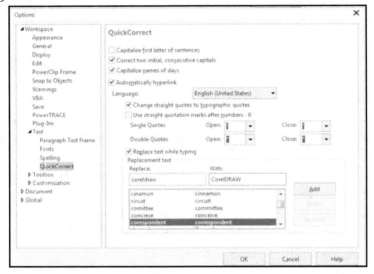

Figure 5.30   Options dialog box

2. Enable the **Replace text while typing** check box.
3. In the **Replace:** box, type the text to be replaced.
4. Type the replacement text in the **With:** box.
5. Click **Add**.

To add spelling corrections to QuickCorrect, do this:

1. Click **Tools** menu and choose **Options...** .
2. In the **Options** dialog box, from the menu on left side, click on the **Workplace** list of categories double-click **Text**, and click **Spelling**.

3. Check the Perform Automatic Spell Checking check box. (See Figure 5.31)
4. Spell check will be done automatically, as you type the text. Or
5. Enable the Add corrections to QuickCorrect check box.

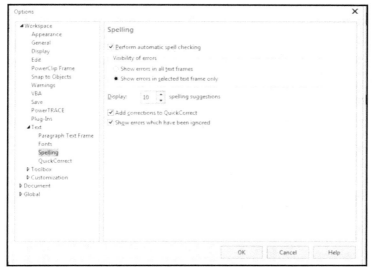

Figure 5.31 Selecting Add corrections to QuickCorrect and automatic spell checking in Options dialog box

CHAPTER 6

Advanced Text Work

Fitting Text to Path

You can position artistic text along the path of an open object (for example, a line) or a closed object (for example, a square).

After you fit text to a path, you can adjust the text's position relative to that path. For example, you can place the text horizontally, vertically or both. You can adjust the distance between the text and the path.

To add text along a path, do this:

1. Using the **Pick** tool, select a path.
2. Click Te<u>x</u>t menu and choose Fit <u>T</u>ext to path as shown in Figure 6.1.

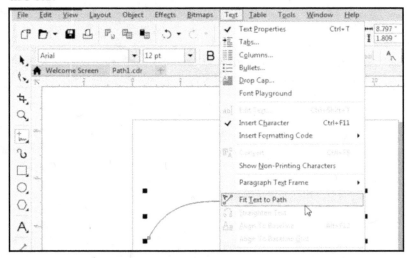

Figure 6.1   Selecting Fit Text to Path in the Text menu

3. The text cursor is inserted on the path. If the path is open, the text cursor is inserted at the beginning of the path. If the path is closed, the text cursor is inserted at the center of the path.
4. Type along the path.

To fit text to a path, do this:

1. Draw a Curve using the Freehand tool.

2. Click **Text** menu and choose **Fit Text to path**.

3. The pointer changes to the **Fit text to path** pointer ↗. By moving the pointer over the path, you can preview where the text will be fitted.

4. Type along the path. If the text is fitted to a closed path, the text is centered along the path. If the text is fitted to an open path, the text flows from the point of insertion (See Figure 6.2).

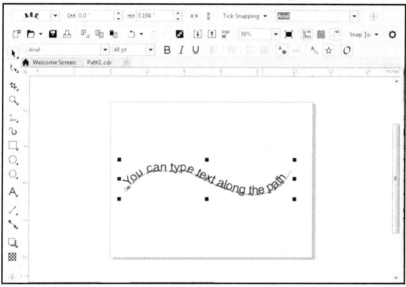

Figure 6.2   Fitting text to path

5. On the property bar as shown in Figure 6.3, choose from the following options:

Text orientation Distance from path   Offset Mirror text horizontally

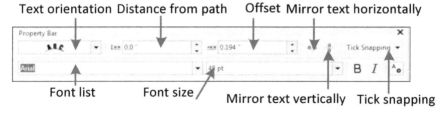

Font list   Font size   Mirror text vertically   Tick snapping

Figure 6.3   Property bar

Text Orientation — click the drop down list and choose the text bends to follow the path.

Distance from path — click the list box and choose to specify the distance between the text and the path. You can move your text above (give value in the box) or below the path.

Horizontal Offset — click the list box and choose to specify the distance by which you want to move the text along the path horizontally. You can move your text left (give value in the box) or right the path.

Mirror Horizontally — It flips the text characters from left to right.

Mirror Vertically — It flips the text characters upside down.

Tick Spacing — To increase the distance between the path and the text, click the arrow, enable tick snapping on option, and type a value in the **Tick spacing:** box.

You can also change the horizontal position of fitted text by selecting it with the Shape tool, and dragging the character nodes you want to reposition.

Using the Pick tool, you can move text along the path by dragging the small red node that appears beside the text.

Note: If the text is fitted to a closed path, the text is centered along the path. If the text is fitted to an open path, the text flows from the point of insertion. You cannot fit text to the path of another text object. You can also fit text to a path by clicking the Text tool, pointing over an object, clicking where you want the text to begin, and typing the text.

CorelDRAW X8 treats text fitted to a path as one object. However, you can separate the text from the object if you no longer want it to be part of the path. When you separate text from a curved or closed path, the text retains the shape of the object to which it was fitted. Straightening reverts the text to its original appearance.

To separate text from a path do this:

1. Select the fitted text using the **Pick** tool.
2. Click **Object** menu and choose **Break Text Apart** or **Ctrl + K** (See Figure 6.4)

To straighten text, do this:

1. Select the fitted text using the Pick tool.
2. Separate the text from the path.
3. Click **Text** menu and choose **Straighten Text**. (See Figure 6.5)

Figure 6.4   The text separated from the path

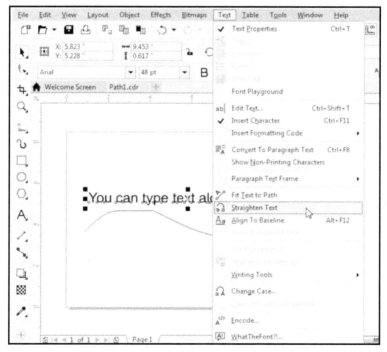

Figure 6.5   The separated text straighten out

Wrapping Text within an Object

You can change the shape of text by wrapping paragraph text around an object, artistic text, or a text frame. You can wrap text by using contour or square wrapping styles. The contour wrapping styles follow the curve of the object. The square wrapping styles follow the bounding box of the object. You can also adjust the amount of space between paragraph text and the object or text.

To wrap paragraph text around an object, artistic text or text frame, do this:

1. Select the object or text around which you want to wrap text.

2. Click **Window** menu highlight **Docker** and choose **Object Properties**. The **Object Properties** docker window opens.

3. Click the **Summary** button ![icon] to display the wrap options.

4. Click the **Wrap paragraph text** drop-down and choose the desired option from the wrapping style list box. For example, here we select **Contour Flows Left** text as shown in Figure 6.6.

5. Type the offset amount in the **Text wrap offset** list box. This is the distance between the object and text.

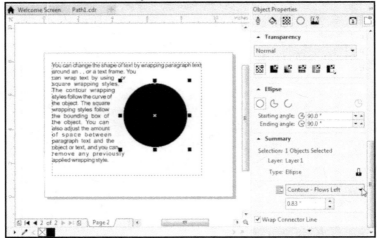

Figure 6.6 Applying Contour Flows left style of wrapping text

Untext

What do we mean by untext? It is the text that is no longer treated as text by CorelDRAW X8.

To untext the text, do this:

1. Click the Text tool.
2. Select the text, which you want to untext.
3. Click Object menu and choose Con**v**ert to Curves or press Ctrl+Q keys together.

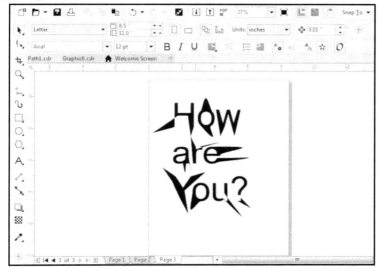

Figure 6.7 The word is distorted using Shape tool

4. Click the Shape tool and drag the node, the word is distorted (See Figure 6.7).

Kerning a Range of Characters

Individual adjustment of characters is called kerning. To kern characters means to adjust the space between the characters. Capital letters often need manual kerning to look better.

To kern characters, do this:

1. Select the characters with Text tool you want to kern.
2. Click the Te**x**t menu and choose Text **P**roperties or Ctrl+T keys.
3. In the Character Formatting docker click Range kerning: list box to set a value for kerning. Or
4. Select the text, switch to the Shape tool, and drag the small thingamabob (i.e. the area enclosed by a rectangle with a drop shadow) in or out, as shown in Figure 6.8.

Figure 6.8 Kerning text with the shape tool

CorelDRAW X8 carries with it the built-in intelligence to adjust the kerning. It understands which character combinations need more space among them and which need less. This is referred to as kerning pairs. Invariably, however, text at large sizes or in all caps needs to be scrutinized for proper kerning. Figure 6.9 shows various types of kerning.

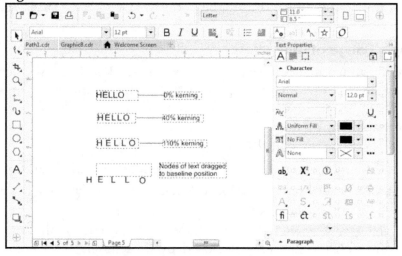

Figure 6.9 Different types of kerning

Working with Text Styles

CorelDRAW provides advanced style capabilities that allow you to format document text with speed, ease, and consistency. A style is a collection of formatting attributes defining object properties, such as artistic and paragraph text properties. For example, to define a character style, you can specify font type, font style and size, text color and background color, character position, caps, and more. You can create styles and style sets for text.

You can create and apply styles and style sets to different types of objects: graphic objects, artistic and paragraph text, callout and dimension objects, and any objects created with the Artistic Media tools.

Creating styles and style sets

CorelDRAW lets you group styles into style sets. A style set is a collection of styles that helps you define the appearance of an object. For example, you can create a style set containing a fill style and an outline style that you can apply to graphic objects such as rectangles, ellipses, and curves

There are two options for creating styles. You can create a style or style set based on the formatting of an object that you like, or you can create a style or style set from scratch by setting the object attributes in the Object styles docker.

To create a style from an object, do this:

1. Select the object you want to create a style.
2. Using the **Pick** tool, right-click an object.
3. Choose **Object** **S**tyles, a sub menu appears choose **New** **S**tyle from, and point to a style type such as Outline, Fill and Transparency. For example, here we select Outline. Or
4. Click **W**indows menu highlight **D**ockers, and select **Object** **S**tyles. Alternatively, press **Ctrl+F5** keys together.
5. The **New style From** dialog box appears, type a name in the **New Style Name**: box as shown in Figure 6.10.
6. In **Object Styles** docker window, choose **Outline width** and **color** to change the Object attributes.

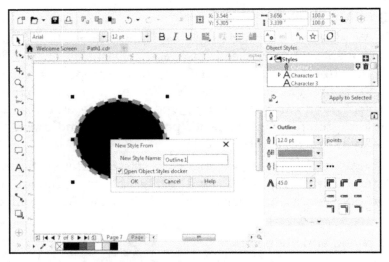

Figure 6.10 Create New Style from dialog box

7. A preview shows you what object attributes will be included in the new style as shown in Figure 6.10.

Note: When you create a style from an existing object, CorelDRAW does not automatically apply the style to the object. If you want the object to use the style, you must apply the style.

To define a style, do this:

1. Choose **Object Styles,** a sub menu appears choose **New style,** button and point to a style type such as Outline, Fill and Transparency. For example, here we select Character. Or

2. Click **Windows** menu highlight **Dockers,** and select **Object Styles.** Alternatively, press **Ctrl+F5** keys together.

3. The style appears in the **Styles** folder with a name assigned by the application, for example "**Character 1**″ as shown in Figure 6.11.

4. Specify the style attributes that you want in the paragraph text frame. For example, here we apply a style font type and font size.

5. Click **Apply to selected** button. The selected font type and size applied in the paragraph as shown in Figure 6.12.

To delete a style do this:

1. Select the style you want to delete.

2. Right click and **Delete.**

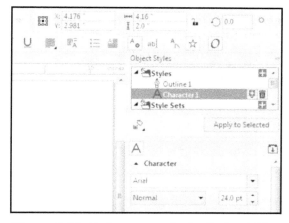

Figure 6.11 Styles appear in the Styles folder

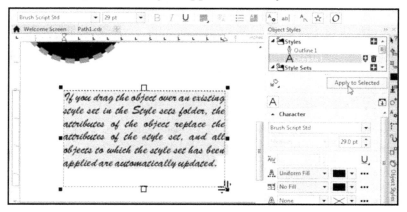

Figure 6.12 Style attributes in the paragraph text frame

3. Select a style in the Styles folder, and click the Delete style button.

To rename a style, do this:

1. Select the style you want to rename.
2. Right-click a style, click Rename, type a new name, and press enter.

To define a style set, do this:

1. Click Windows menu highlight Dockers, and select Object Styles. Alternatively, press Ctrl+F5 keys together.

2. In the **Object styles** docker, click the **New style set** button to create an empty style set to which you can add styles.

3. The style set appears in the **Style sets** folder with a name assigned by the application, for example "**Style Set 1**" in the Object Styles docker window as shown in Figure 6.13.

Figure 6.13 Style Set 1 folder create in the Style Sets folder

4. Specify the style attributes that you want in the paragraph text frame. For example, here we apply a style font type in the Character and center align in the Paragraph properties as shown in Figure 6.14.

5. Click **Apply to selected** button. The selected font type and center alignment applied in the Style Sets folder shown in Figure 6.14.

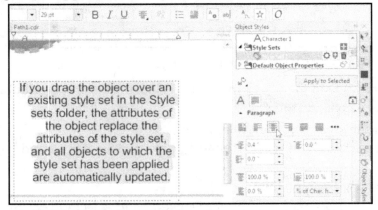

Figure 6.14 Define a style set in the Styles Sets folder

Linking Paragraph Text Frames

Linking frames enables or directs the flow of text from one text frame to another to incase the amount of text that exceeds the size of the first text frame. However, shrinking or enlarging a linked paragraph text frame or changing the size of the text automatically adjusts the amount of text in the next text frame. You can also create and link paragraph text frames before you begin typing text in the first text frame.

You can link a paragraph text frame to an open or closed object. When you link a paragraph text frame to an open object (for example, a line), the text flows along the path of the line. Linking a text frame to a closed object (for example, a rectangle) inserts a paragraph text frame and directs the flow of text inside the object. If text exceeds the open or closed path, you can link it to another text frame or object. You can also link to paragraph text frames and objects across pages.

After linking paragraph text frames, you can redirect the flow from one object or text frame to another. When you select the text frame or object, a blue arrow indicates the direction of the text flow. You can also hide or display the arrows that indicate the direction of the text flow.

If all the text does not fit in a single frame, then you can flow it from one frame to another. This technique is essential for laying out presentation and documents that arrange text in multiple frames.

To Flow Text from one frame into another, do this:

1. Select a text frame using the Pick tool.

   Drag up on the bottom handle (not the shape-sizing handle). Keep making your text frame smaller until, not all the text you typed fits into the frame. When text does not fit in the frame, the bottom sizing handle changes from an open square to one with a triangle in it. (See Figure 6.15)

2. Use the Text tool in the toolbox to draw a new text frame.

3. Click the Text flow tab ⬜ at the bottom of the text frame or object. If the text frame cannot hold all the text, the tab contains an arrow ▼ and the text frame becomes red as shown in Figure 6.15.

4. When the pointer changes to a **Link to** pointer ▤↘, do one of the following:

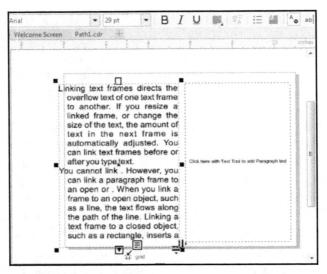

Figure 6.15 Clicking the Text flow tab changes to link pointer

- To link to a frame or object on the same page, click the text frame or object into which you want to continue the text flow.

- To link to an existing frame or object on a different page, click the corresponding **Page** tab on the document navigator, and then click the text frame or object.

- To create a new linked frame on another page, click the corresponding **Page** tab on the document navigator, and hover over the area of the drawing page that corresponds to the position of the first frame. When a preview of the frame appears, click to create the linked frame. The new frame has the same size and position as the original frame. If you click elsewhere on the page, the text frame that is created is the size of the entire page

5. Point to the new text frame into which you will continue the text. A large black arrow appears, as shown in Figure 6.16.

6. Click to pour the overflow text into the new frame. After you continue text, the bottom handle of the first frame displays a box with lines, meaning this text is continued. A line appears connecting the original frame to the "continued to" frame, as shown in Figure 6.16.

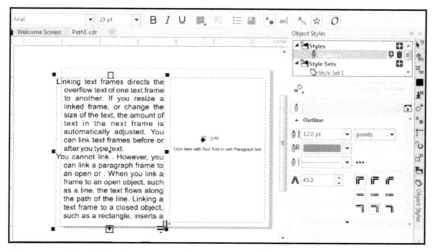

Figure 6.16 A black arrow indicating text flow into the new text frame

7. Enlarge your second text frame until all the continued text fits. When there is no more text to display, the bottom handle of the final frame is displayed as an open square as shown in Figure 6.17.

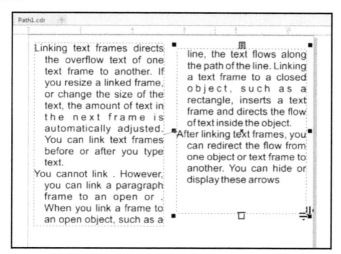

Figure 6.17 Flow of text continued to next frame

To remove links between text frames or objects, do this:

1. Using the **Pick** tool, select the linked frames or objects.

2. Click the **Text** menu highlight **Paragraph Text Frame** and choose Unlink as shown in Figure 6.18.

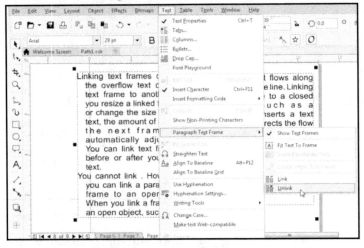

Figure 6.18 Unlink a between link frames

To specify formatting preferences for text frames, do this:

1. Click **Tools** menu and choose **Options**… . Alternatively, press **Ctrl + J** keys together.

2. The **Options** dialog box appears as shown in Figure 6.19.

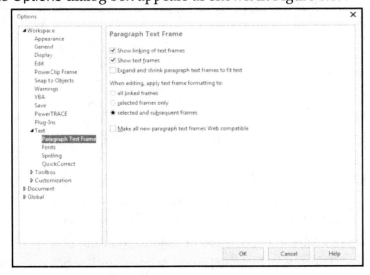

Figure 6.19 Options dialog box

3. In the Workspace list of categories, double-click Text, and click Paragraph Text Frame.

4. If you want to hide or display the text flow indicators, disable or enable the Show linking of text frames check box.

5. In the When editing, apply paragraph frames formatting to area, enable one of the following options:

   • All linked frames — It applies paragraph formatting to selected text frames and all text frames that are linked to them.

   • Selected frames only — It applies paragraph formatting to the selected text frames only

   • Selected and subsequent frames — It applies paragraph formatting to selected text frames and any text frames that are later linked to them.

6. Display and hide text frames, Enable the Show text frames check box.

7. Enable automatic expanding and shrinking of frames to fit text, enable the Expand and shrink paragraph text frames to fit text check box.

8. Click the desired setting you want to changes in the paragraph text frame options and click OK button.

CHAPTER 7

Working with Layers and Symbols

Working with Layers

CorelDRAW X8 allows you to arrange elements in complex drawings using Layering. Layering technique helps in organizing a drawing and you can divide a drawing into multiple layers. Each layer will contain a portion of the drawing's contents. You can apply changes to a portion of the drawing without affecting the rest.

Each new file has one master page, which contains and controls the default layers. These are:

- **Guides**, this layer contains the guidelines that you set up stores page-specific (local) guidelines.

- **Layer 1**, represents the default local layer. When you draw objects on the page, the objects are added to this layer unless you choose a different layer.

The Master Page contains the information that applies to all pages in a document. You can add one or more layers to a master page to hold content such as headers, footers, or a static background. By default, a master page contains the following layers:

- **Guides (all pages)** — contains the guidelines that are used for all pages of the document. All objects placed on the Guides layer appear as outlines only, and the outlines act as guidelines.

- **Desktop** — contains objects that are outside the borders of the drawing page. This layer lets you store objects that you may want to include in the drawing at a later time.

- **Document grid** — contains the document grid that is used for all pages of the document. The document grid is always the bottom layer.

To add content to a layer, you must first select the layer so that it becomes the active layer. The default layers on the master page cannot be deleted or copied.

To create layer do this:

1. Click **Object** menu and choose **Object Manager**. The **Object Manager** Docker window appears as shown in Figure 7.1.

Figure 7.1 The Object Manager Docker Window

2. To create a new layer, click the small triangle at the top-right corner of the window. *Alternatively*, you can right click on any open space in the Docker window.

3. Select <u>New</u> Layer from the pop-up menu (See Figure 7.2).

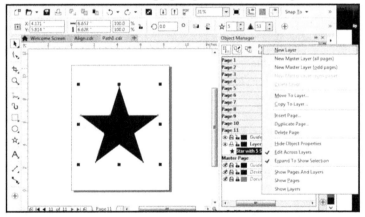

Figure 7.2 Adding new layer from the Object Manager Docker window

Layers Properties

A layer has three basic properties that you can control. These properties can be controlled through the docker window only. You can see in the docker window that each layer is accompanied by three icons namely **eyes**, **print** and **Lock**. These icons can be used to control the layer properties.

Icon	Layer Property	Description
(eye icon)	Visibility	Click the eye to make a layer show or hide layers
(printer icon)	Printability	Click the printer icon on the docker window to set the printing and exporting properties for a layer to control whether a layer is displayed in the printed or exported drawing
(pencil/lock icon)	Editability	Click the pencil icon to lock or unlock a layer. Locking a layer means that no activity can take place on it at all

To move an object between layers, do this:

1. Select the object and click the small triangle at the top right corner of the window.
2. From the menu that appears, choose <u>M</u>ove To Layer....
3. Click the layer to which you want to move the object.
4. In the layers list, drag a layer name to a new position.

You can change the order of the master layers relative to local layers by displaying the list of all layers for the current page and dragging a layer name to a new position in the layers list. To display all layers for a page, click

a page name, click the Layer manager *view button* (icon) *at the top of the* Object manager *docker, and choose* Current page, layers only.

To copy a layer, do this:

1. In the object manager docker window layers list, right-click the layer that you want to copy a layer, click **Copy**.
2. Right-click the layer above which you want to place the copied layer, click **Paste**.

The layer and the objects it contains are pasted above the selected layer.

To delete a layer, do this:

1. In the docker window, right click the layer which you want to delete.

2. From the menu that appears choose <u>D</u>elete.

To display or hide a layer, do this:

1. In the docker window, click the **Eye** icon beside the layer name.
2. The layer is hidden when the **Eye** icon is grayed.

Object Locking

The Object Locking features make the selected object untouchable, even if the layer it resides on it is editable. Locking an object will restrict any further modification on the object.

To lock an object, do this:

1. Click the **Object** menu highlight. A sub menu appears choose **<u>L</u>ock Object**. *Alternatively*, right click and choose **<u>L</u>ock Object** command from the Shortcut menu.
2. The handles around the object change to little lock symbols as shown around the star in Figure 7.3.

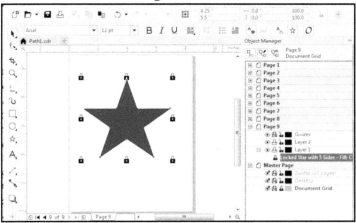

Figure 7.3 Locked object

Now, you cannot *move, resize, rotate, recolor* or *delete* the Star. The object remains as it is till you unlock it.

To unlock an object, do this:

1. Select the object you want to unlock.
2. Click **Object** menu highlight **<u>L</u>ock**. A sub menu options appears choose **Unloc<u>k</u> object**.

Now you can modify, copy or delete these objects as needed.

To change the layer color, do this:

1. In the **Object manager** docker, double-click the color swatch that appears to the left of the layer name; choose a color from **Select** color dialog box.

Working with Symbols

CorelDRAW X8, you create objects and save them as symbols. Symbols are defined once and can be referenced many times in a drawing. Each time you insert a symbol into a drawing, you create an instance of the symbol. Symbol definitions, as well as information about instances, are stored in a symbol manager, which is part of the CorelDRAW (CDR) file. Using symbols for objects that appear many times in a drawing helps to reduce the file size.

Symbols are created from objects. When you convert an object to a symbol, the new symbol is added to the **Symbol manager**, and the selected object becomes an instance. Any changes you make will affect all instances in a drawing. The selection handles for symbols differ from those for objects. Selection handles for symbols are blue; selection handles for objects are black.

To convert an object to a symbol, do this:

1. Select an object or multiple objects.

2. Click **Object** menu and choose **Symbol**. A sub menu appears, select **New Symbol**... .

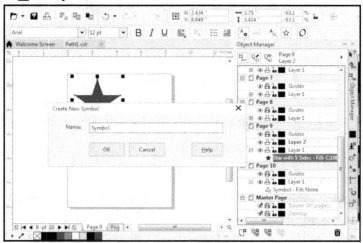

Figure 7.4 Create New Symbol dialog box

3. **Create New Symbol** dialog box appears as shown in Figure 7.4. Here, you have to give the name of the symbol in the **Name**: list box.

4. The **Symbol** name appears under the **Layers** in the **Object Manager**.

5. Click OK.

Note: Symbols cannot span layers. If you convert objects on different layers to a symbol, the objects are combined on the topmost object's layer as shown in the docker window of Figure 7.4.

To rename a symbol, do this:

1. Click **Object** menu choose **Symbol**, a sub menu appears, select **Symbol manager**. Alternatively, press **Ctrl+F3** keys together. Symbol Manager docker window appears as shown in Figure 7.5.

2. If you want to name or rename the symbol, double-click the symbol's name box, and type a name. (See Figure 7.5)

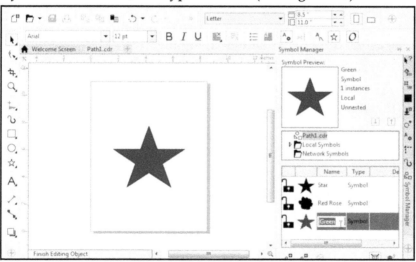

Figure 7.5 Renaming the symbol in the symbol manager

To edit a symbol, do this:

1. Select the symbol on the drawing window in the Symbol Manager. (See Figure 7.6)

2. Click the **Edit Symbol** button on the bottom of the docker window.

3. Modify the objects on the drawing page. (See Figure 7.6)

4. After that click on the **Finish editing object** tab in the bottom left corner of the drawing window.

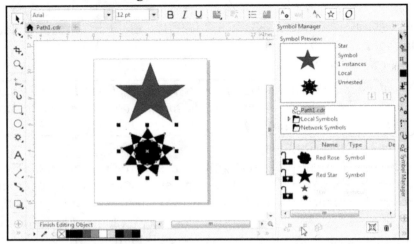

Figure 7.6 Editing a symbol in the drawing window

5. Changes made to a symbol are automatically made to all instances in the active drawing as shown in Figure 7.7.

*You can also edit a symbol by selecting an instance in the drawing window and clicking the **Edit symbol** button* 🔳 *on the property bar, or holding down **Ctrl** and clicking a symbol instance.*

To delete a symbol, do this:

1. In the **Symbol manger** docker, choose a symbol from the list.

2. Click the **Delete symbol** button 🔳.

When you delete a symbol, all instances of the symbol are removed from the drawing.

To insert a symbol instance, do this:

1. In the **Symbol manager** docker window, select the symbol from the symbol list.

2. If you want the symbol scaled automatically to match the current drawing scale, enable the **Scale to world units** button. (See Figure 7.8)

3. Choose the symbol from the list.

4. Click the **Insert symbol** button. (See Figure 7.8)

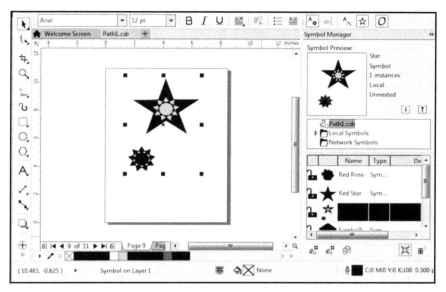

Figure 7.7 Changes applied in the instance of the symbol

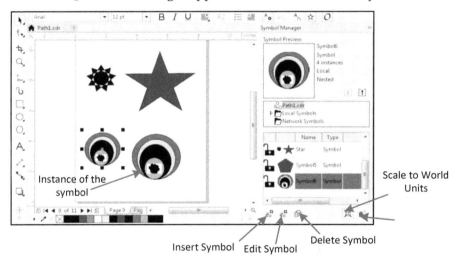

Instance of the symbol

Scale to World Units

Insert Symbol   Edit Symbol

Delete Symbol

Figure 7.8 Insert a symbol instance

To convert a symbol instance to an object or objects, do this:

1. Select a symbol instance.

2. Click Object menu highlight Symbol. A sub menu appears, select Revert to objects.

Working with Layers and Symbols   **139**

CHAPTER 8

Outline Tool

Introduction

An outline is the visible line that wraps around an object i.e. comes around an object. You can change the appearance of both lines and outlines by using the controls in the **Outline** section of the **Object properties** docker, the **Outline pen** dialog box, and the property bar. You can quickly define outlines from the Property Bar or in more detail from the **Outline Tool** flyout. You can set the *width, style, color* and *attributes* of outlines using the outline flyout. The outline tool flyout is shown in Figure 8.1.

You can choose a corner style to control the corner shape in lines and choose a line cap style to change the appearance of a line's endpoints. By default, an outline is applied on top of an object's fill, but you can apply it behind the fill, with the fill overlapping the outline. You can also link the outline thickness to an object's size so that the outline increases when you increase the object's size and decreases when you decrease the object's size.

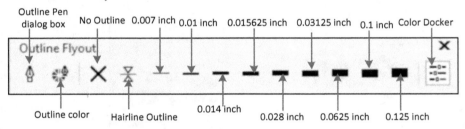

Figure 8.1 The Outline tool flyout

Using the Outline Pen Dialog Box

To set the outline details you will need to use the **Outline Pen** dialog box. Outline dialog box offers many features for outlining objects. You can also use the Outline box to set the *width, line style, color, line ends, line caps,* etc.

Setting Outline

To specify outline settings, do this:

1. Select the object for which you want to define settings.

2. Click the **Outline tool** flyout and choose the first tool in the flyout. *Alternatively*, press **F12**, key on your keyboard.

3. The **Outline Pen** dialog box appears as shown in Figure 8.2. Or

4. Click the **Window** menu highlight **Dockers**, a sub menu appears select **Object Properties**. Alternatively, press **Alt+Enter** keys together.

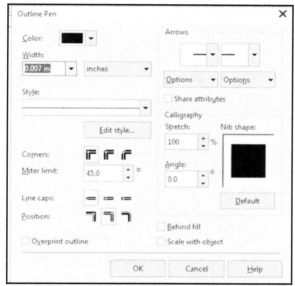

Figure 8.2   The Outline Pen dialog box

You can also changes of a selected object from the Outline pen dialog box or Object Properties docker window.

Outline Width

1. In the **Outline Pen** dialog box, click on the **Width:** drop down list and choose a width and unit of measurement for drawing the outline.

2. Click Ok. *Alternatively*, the outline width can be set from the preset buttons in the Outline tool flyout.

To set Outline width from the preset buttons, do this:

1. Select the object using **Pick tool**, the width of outline of which you want to change.

2. Click the **Outline tool** in the toolbox. or

3. Choose from one of the Preset buttons. You can choose thickness range from hairline width to 10 point thickness (See Figure 8.3).

4. In the **Outline** section, type a value or click the drop-down arrow button in the **Width** box (See Figure 8.3).

5. The thickness will be applied to the outline of the selected circle object.

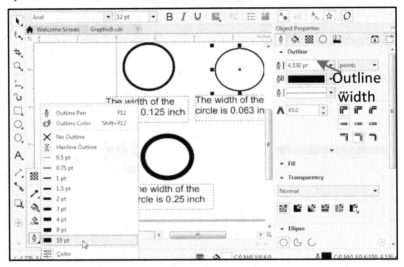

Figure 8.3   Choosing Outline width from the preset button of Outline tool flyout

Outline Styles

To set outline styles, do this:

1. In the **Outline Pen** dialog box, choose a line from the **Style** drop down list (See Figure 8.4) or.

2. In the docker window, select **Line Style** from the **Outline** section as shown in Figure 8.4.

3. You can choose *Solid, Dash* like or *dot* like line styles from this list (See Figure 8.4). You can also create line styles of your choice.

To create your own line style, do this:

1. In the **Outline Pen** dialog box, choose a style other than solid line, from the **Style:** drop down list.

2. Click on the **Edit Style...** button. **Edit Line Style** dialog box appears as shown in Figure 8.5.

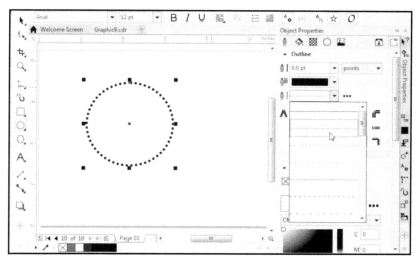

Figure 8.4   Choosing line style for the Outline

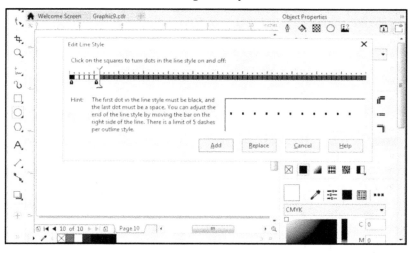

Figure 8.5   Editing line style to create a new line style

3. In the **Object Properties,** click the **Settings** ■ ■ ■ button to create a line style in the **Edit line style** dialog box.

4. In the **Edit Line Style** dialog box, move the vertical bar to the right or to the left for turning the dots on the line *ON* or *OFF*. By clicking the boxes to the left of the slider, you can specify the placement and frequency of the dots in the new line style you create.

5. Click <u>A</u>dd button. The changes applied in the line style.

6. If you open with **Outline Pen** dialog box makes changes and click OK button.

Outline Color

To set color to the outline, do this:

1. In the **Outline Pen** dialog box, choose a color for the outline from the **Color:** drop down box as shown in Figure 8.6.

2. Select the color from the color viewers. After you select the color click OK button in the **Outline Pen** dialog box. Or

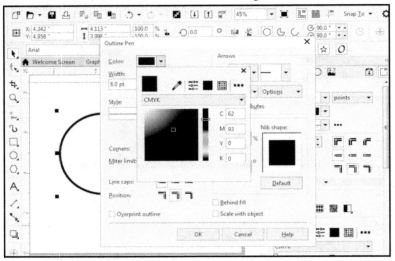

Figure 8.6 Selecting color for the outline from the Color drop down list

3. Click the **Outline** flyout and choose select **Outline Color.** Alternatively press **Shift+F12** keys together.

4. The **Select Color** dialog box appears as shown in Figure 8.7. Here you can change the *palettes, choose spot colors* and also you can mix your own CMYK, RGB or HSB colors.

5. Click OK.

Outline Corners

To set Outline corners, do this:

1. Select the object for which you want to set outline corners.

2. Click the **Outline tool** flyout and choose **Outline Pen** dialog tool.

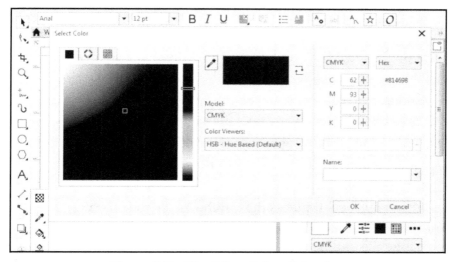

Figure 8.7 The Select Color dialog box

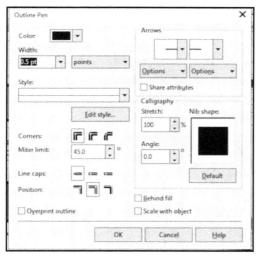

Figure 8.8 Select the corner type of your choice

3. In the **Outline Pen** dialog box, from the **Corners**: area choose a corner type for your outline as shown in Figure 8.8

4. Click OK. Or **you can also**

5. In the **Object Properties**, choose a unit of measurement from the **Outline units** box to change the units of measurement for the outline width.

6. To set the miter limit type a value in the **Miter limit:** box to set the angle at which the shape of sharp angles.

7. Click one of the following buttons to set the shape of corners:

   - **Mitered corners** — It creates pointed corners
   - **Round corners** — It creates rounded corners
   - **Beveled corners** — It creates squared off corners

8. Click one of the following buttons to specify the outline position.

   - **Outside outline** — It places the outline outside the object
   - **Centered outline** — centers the outline along the object edge
   - **Inside outline** — It places the outline inside the object

9. The shape of rectangle corners and position in the above options to change the outline object as shown in Figure 8.9.

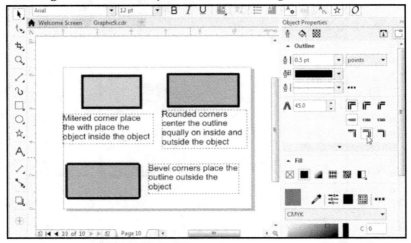

Figure 8.9 Different types of outline corners and positions

Setting Outline Arrows

CorelDRAW X8 lets you define outlines in the form of arrows to your objects. A wide variety of arrows are available and you can choose an arrow style of your choice from the exhaustive range available.

To set and edit arrow at the line ends, do this:

1. Select a line or curve that has an arrowhead.

2. In the **Outline Pen** dialog box, from the **Arrow** area, choose an arrow type of your choice from the two arrow boxes.

3. The arrow box at the left specifies the arrow that will appear at the starting point of the line. The arrow box at the right specifies the arrow for the ending point of your line. Or

4. In the **Object Properties,** click the Outline section, click the Arrowhead settings button ■■■ next to the **Start arrowhead** picker or the **End arrowhead** picker, and click Attributes as shown in Figure 8.10.

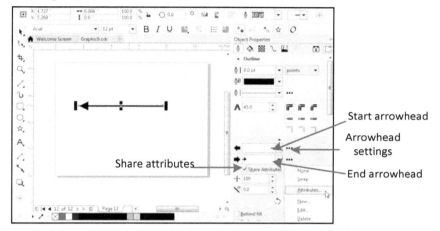

Figure 8.10 Selecting arrowhead in the Object Properties docker window

- If you want starting and ending arrowheads to have the same size, offset, rotation angle, and orientation, enable the **Share attributes** check box.

5. In the **Arrowhead attributes** dialog box appears as shown in Figure 8.11 specify the attributes you want.

6. In the **Size** area, type a value in the **Length:** or **Width:** box to specify the size of an arrowhead. Click the **Proportional** check box to share the same height and width of the object.

7. In the **Mirror** area, enable the **Horizontally** or **Vertically** check box to Mirror an arrowhead to flip the arrowhead horizontal and vertical.

8. In the **Offset** area, type values in the **X:** and **Y:** boxes to offset an arrowhead i.e. the interspace between line and arrowhead as shown in Figure 8.11.

9. Specify an angle in the **Rotation:** box to **Rotate** an arrowhead.

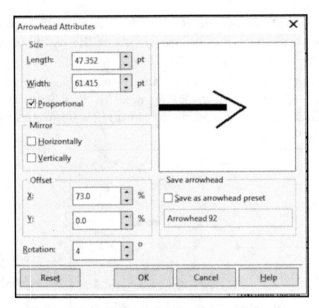

Figure 8.11 Arrowhead Attributes dialog box

10. Enable the **Save as arrowhead preset** check box to save custom arrowhead attributes as an arrowhead preset.

11. After to set the desired setting the different types of arrowhead as shown in Figure 8.12.

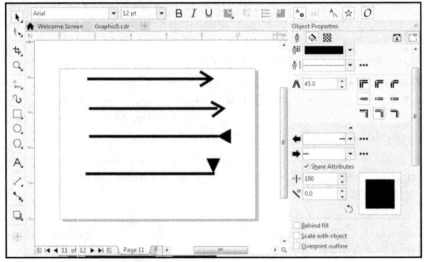

Figure 8.12 Different types of arrowhead

To edit an arrowhead preset, do this:

1. Using the Pick tool, select an object that has an arrowhead.
2. In the Outline section, click the Arrowhead settings button next to the Start arrowhead picker or the End arrowhead picker, and click Edit… .
3. In the Arrowhead attributes dialog box, specify the attributes you want.

To delete an arrowhead preset, do this:

1. To delete an arrowhead preset, select the preset from the Start or End arrowhead picker, click the Arrowhead settings button, and click Delete.

Applying Calligraphic Outlines

Calligraphic lines are similar to the lines drawn using a calligraphic pen. Such lines change their thickness according to the direction of the line. Line's thickness also varies depending upon the angle of the pen nib.

To apply calligraphic effects to your outline do this:

1. In the Outline Pen dialog box, from the Calligraphy area, set values for the Stretch and Angle of the calligraphic pen (See Figure 8.8). Or
2. In the Outline section of Object Properties, type a value in the Stretch box to change the width of the pen's nib.
   - The value range is from 1 to 100, with 100 as the default setting. Reducing the value makes square nibs rectangular and round nibs oval, creating a more pronounced calligraphic effect.
   - Type a value in the Tilt nib: box to change the orientation of the pen in relation to the drawing surface.
3. You can preview your settings in the Tilt Nib shape: box. Fig ure 8.13 shows the difference in the outline with 3 sample settings.
4. Click Apply.

Setting Outline Options with the Property Bar

The property bar that appears when you select a curve object, enables you to define several attributes of that object's outline.

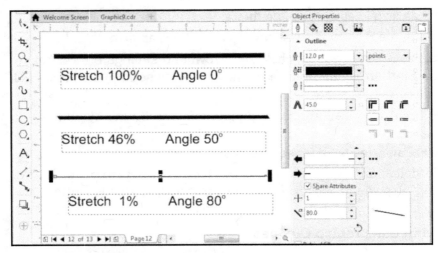

Figure 8.13 Lines with different Calligraphy settings

The different options available with Property Bar are given in Table 8.1.

Table 8.1 Outline tool property bar

Icon	Name	Description
— ▼	Star Arrowhead Selector	Defines the look of the arrow (if any) at the start of the line
————— ▼	Outline Style Selector	Defines look of the outline ranging from dashes and dots to solid lines.
— ▼	End Arrowhead Selector	Defines the look of the arrow at the end of the curve
3.0 pt ▼	Outline Width Selector	Enables you to pick from a larger set of outline widths similar to those available in the Outline flyout

Behind Fill Option

By default, the thickness of the outline extends into the object. That is, half of the thickness of the outline will appear inside the object. If you have applied any fills to your object, the outline will overlap the fills.

To make outline remain behind a fill, do this:

1. In the Outline Pen dialog box, check the Behind fill check box. Or

2. In the Outline section, enable the Behind fill check box, to apply an outline behind an object's fill.

The outline will appear behind the fills that you have applied in the object. (See Figure 8.14) When the object is without any fills this control produces no effect.

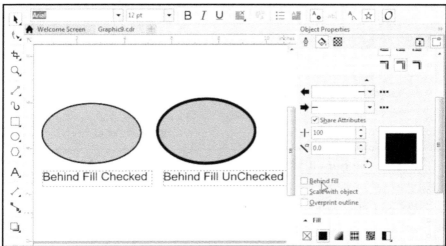

Figure 8.14 Illustrating behind fill option

Scale with Image Option

By default, the outline width will not be set according to the size of the image. For example, suppose you had set the outline width to 8-point thickness. Now if you decreased the object size by 50%, the thickness of your outline will be set according object's size. But you wanted the outline to be proportional to the size of the image.

To scale the outline proportional to image size, do this:

1. In the Outline Pen dialog box, check the Scale with object check box.

2. In the Outline section, enable the Scale with object check box, to link the outline thickness to an object's size.

3. Enable the Overprint outline check box, to set the outline to print on top of underlying colors during printing.

Figure 8.15 shows the effect of decreasing size of object, on its outline, with **Scaling the object** unchecked and checked.

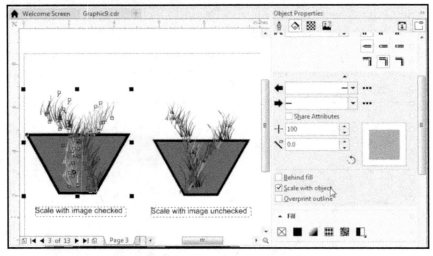

Figure 8.15 Scale with object illustrated

Outline Color

Outline Color helps out to choose fill and outline colors by selecting a color from the Document palette, custom color palettes, palettes from the Palette libraries, color viewers, or color blends. When you want to use a color that already exists in an object or document, you can sample the color by using the Color eyedropper tool to achieve an exact match.

The color palettes that are found in the Palette libraries cannot be edited directly. Some of them are provided by third-party manufacturers. Some examples of these are PANTONE, HKS colors, and TRUMATCH. They are useful when your printer can handle only selected color palettes.

In CorelDRAW, the default color palette is based on the primary color mode of the document. For example, if the document's primary color model is RGB, the default color palette is also RGB.

Color Model

Palettes provide only a fixed number of colors. Using Color model, millions of colors can be generated. Color model represents a formula to produce colors. Colors are generated by mixing the right percentage of different colors.

A common color model is the CMYK color model. An exhaustive range of colors are produced by mixing right percentage of the colors namely, *cyan, magenta, yellow* and *black*.

Color viewers give a representation of a range of colors using one-dimensional or three-dimensional shapes.

To choose a color by using the default color palette, do this:

1. To choose a fill color for a selected object, click a color swatch.
2. To choose an outline color for a selected object, right-click a color swatch.
3. To choose from different shades of a color, click and hold a color swatch to display a pop-up color picker, and then click a color.
4. To view more colors on the default color palette, click the scroll arrows at the top and bottom of the color palette.

To display color names instead of color values, click the **Options** flyout button ▶ at the top of the default palette, and click **Show color names**. This action undocks the default color palette and displays the color names.

To choose a color by using a color palette tab, do this:

1. Select an object.
2. Double-click the **Fill** button ◈ on the status bar.
3. In the **Edit fill** dialog box, click the **Uniform fill** button.
4. Click the **Palettes** ⊞ tab as shown in Figure 8.16.
5. Choose a color palette from the **Palette**: list box as shown in Figure 8.16.
6. Move the color slider to set the range of colors displayed in the color selection area.
7. Click a color in the color selection area.

You can also do:

1. Display or hide the names of colors, enable or disable the **Show color names** check box.

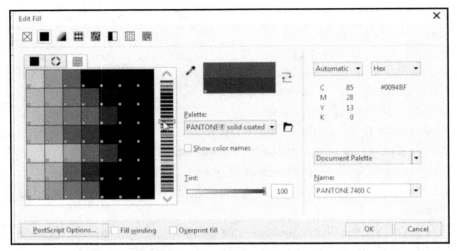

Figure 8.16 Selecting color palette from the Color Palette tab

2. Swap the reference color (original color of the selected object) with the new color, Click the **Swap colors** button.

3. Choose an outline color, double-click the **Outline** button ⌁ on the status bar. In the **Outline pen** dialog box appears, open the **Color picker**, and select in the color selection area.

To choose a color by using a color models tab, do this:

1. Select an object.

2. Double-click the **Fill button** ◈ on the status bar.

3. In the **Edit fill** dialog box, click the **Uniform fill** button.

4. Click the **Models** ■ tab as shown in Figure 8.17.

5. Choose a color model from the **Mod̲el:** list box (See Figure 8.17).

6. Choose a color viewer from the **Color V̲iewers:** list box.

7. Move the color slider.

8. Click a color in the color selection area.

> *You can also access color models in the Color docker by clicking the Show color viewers button and choosing a color model from the list box. If the Color docker is not open, click Window menu highlight Dockers and choose Color.*

Color Harmonies

Color harmonies work by superimposing a shape, such as a rectangle,

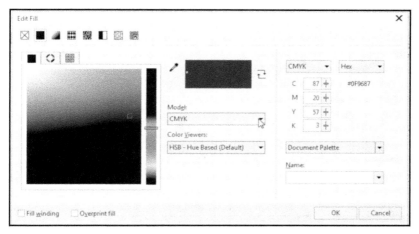

Figure 8.17 Choosing color model from Models tab

pentagon or a triangle over a color wheel. Each vertical row in the color grid begins with the color located at one of the points on the superimposed shape.

The colors at opposite corners of the shape are always complementary, contrasting, or harmonious, depending on the shape you choose. The color harmonies are most useful when you are choosing several colors for a project.

To choose a color by using color harmonies, do this:

1. Select an object.

2. Double-click the Fill button on the status bar.

3. In the **Edit fill** dialog box, click the **Uniform fill** button.

4. Click the **Mixers** tab.

5. Choose **Color Harmonies** from the **Mixers**: list box as shown in Figure 8.18.

6. You can change the cell size of the color grid by moving the **Size**: slider.

7. Choose a shape from the **Hues** list box. You will see the shape on the color wheel.

8. Choose an option from the **Variation**: list box.

9. Click a color swatch on the color palette below the color wheel.

10. When you have selected the color you chosen, click OK.

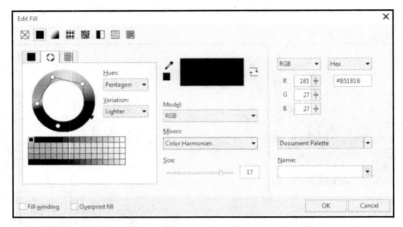

Figure 8.18 Choosing color harmonies from mixers tab

To choose a color by using a color blend, do this:

1. Select an object.

2. Double-click the Fill button on the status bar.

3. In the Edit fill dialog box, click the Uniform fill button.

4. Click the Mixers tab.

5. Choose **Color blend** from the **Mixers**: list box (See Figure 8.19).

6. Choose the color **Mod_el**: drop-down list.

7. Pick a color in the color selection area.

8. You can change the cell size of the color grid by moving the **Size**: slider.

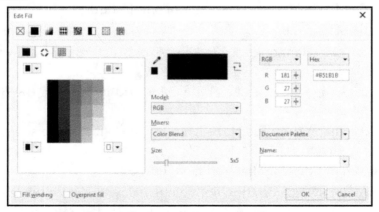

Figure 8.19 Choosing color blend from mixers tab

CHAPTER 9

Fill Tool

Introduction

There are a number of tasks that are common to all types of fills. You can choose a default fill color so that every object that you add to a drawing has the same fill. You can also remove a fill, copy it to another object, or use it to fill an area surrounded by an open curve. If you want to apply the same fill to other objects with fill attributes, you can save the fill settings as a style.

To choose a default fill color, do this:

1. Click a blank area on the drawing page to deselect all objects.

2. On the status bar, double-click the Fill icon ◈.

3. In the Edit fill dialog box appears, choose a fill type, choose a fill color, and click OK.

To remove a fill, do this:

1. Select an object.

2. Click **Object** menu and choose **Object Properties**. Alternatively press **Alt + Enter** keys together.

3. In the **Object properties** docker, click the **No fill button** ⊠.

To copy a fill to another object, do this:

1. Using the **Pick** tool, select the object from which you want to copy the fill.

2. With the right mouse button, drag the object over the destination object to which you want to apply the fill.

3. A blue outline of the first object follows the pointer to the destination object.

4. When the pointer changes to a crosshair pointer ⊕, release the mouse button, and choose **Copy Fill Here** from the context menu as shown in Figure 9.1.

*You can also click the **Interactive fill** tool, select the object to which you want to copy a fill, click the **Copy fill** button on the property bar, and click the object from which you want to copy the fill.*

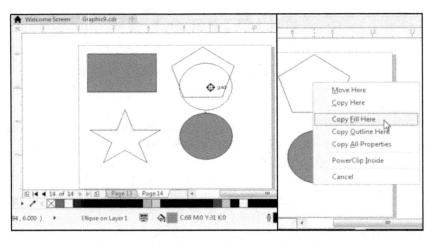

Figure 9.1   Copy a fill to another object

To show fills in open curves, do this:

1. Click **Tools** menu and choose **Options**… . Alternatively, press Ctrl+J keys together.

2. The **Options** dialog box appears. In the left side, a list of categories options appears double-click **Document** and then click **General**.

3. Enable the **Fill open curves** check box. For example, here we have drawn an open path curve as shown in Figure 9.2.

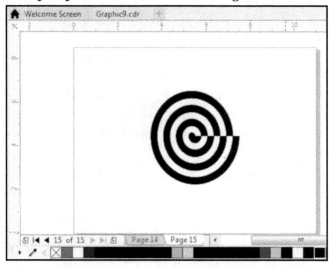

Figure 9.2   Fill color in open curves

Using Uniform Fills

Uniform fill consists of a single solid color filled inside an object. CorelDRAW X8 lets you add uniform fill to an object. CorelDRAW X8 provides various types of fills that are explained in Table 9.1 and also shown in Figure 9.3.

Table 9.1   The different types of fills and their description

Fill	Description
Uniform	A single color or shade that fills the entire object.
Fountain	A fountain fill is a smooth progression of two or more colors that adds depth to an object.
Patterns	An object is filled with a repeating pattern. The pattern can be a color or some bitmapped image.
Textures	Randomly generated fill that gives the object a natural look.
Mesh	Fill consisting of patches of color inside the object.

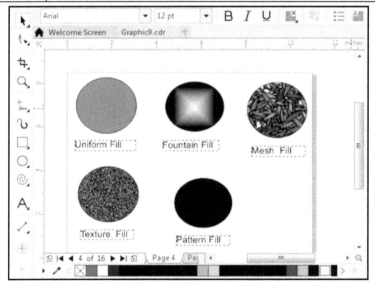

Figure 9.3   Various types of fills

To apply a uniform fill, do this:

1. Select an object.

2. Click a color on the color palette. To mix colors, hold **Ctrl** key and click on the colors in the color palette.

3. You can also choose a uniform fill by clicking

- The **Uniform fill** ■ button in the **Fill** section of the **Object Properties** docker. You can also fill an object by clicking on a color on the color palette, located at the right of the drawing window (See Figure 9.4).

- The **Interactive fill tool** ◈ in the toolbox, and then clicking the **Uniform fill** button on the property bar.

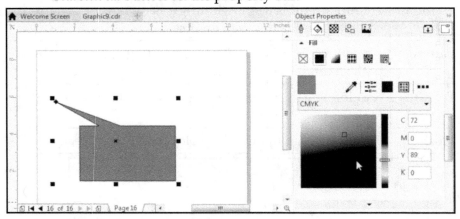

Figure 9.4 Choosing Uniform fill for the selected object

Using Fountain Fills

In Fountain fills, the colors or shades gradually change inside the object. There are four types of fountain fills: *linear, Elliptical, conical* and *Rectangular* (See Figure 9.5).

To apply a fountain fill, do this:

1. Select an object.

2. Click **Object** menu and choose **Object Properties**.

3. In the **Object properties** docker, click the **Fountain fill button** ▨ to display fountain fill options.

4. Open the **Fill** picker, and click a fill thumbnail.

5. Click the **Apply** button ▨ in the pop-up window that appears as shown in Figure 9.5.

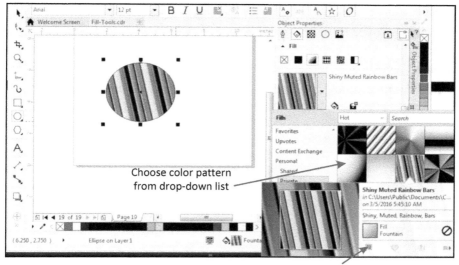

Figure 9.5 Apply Fountain fill in the fountain options list

To create a fountain fill, do this:

1. Select an object.
2. Click **Object** menu and choose **Object Properties**.
3. In the **Object properties** docker, click the **Fountain fill button** ▓ to display fountain fill options.
4. Click one of the following buttons to choose a fountain fill type:

    *   **Linear fountain fill**–Linear fountain fills flows in a straight line across the object.
    *   **Elliptical fountain fill**–A Elliptical fountain fill radiates from the center of the object.
    *   **Conical fountain fill**–Conical fountain fills circles from the center of the object.
    *   **Rectangular fountain fill**–A rectangular fountain fill is dispersed in concentric squares from the center of the object.

5. Click the start node above the color band, open the **Node color** picker, and choose a color.
6. Click the end node above the color band, open the **Node color** picker, and choose a color.

7. Move the midpoint slider below the color band to set the midpoint between the two colors.

8. Select the corresponding node, open the **Node color** picker, and choose a color to change a color.

9. The different types of fountain fill as shown in Figure 9.6.

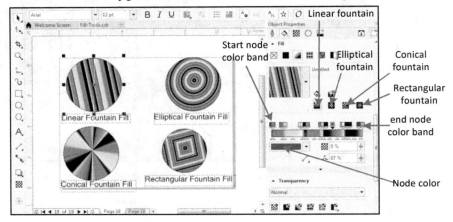

Figure 9.6 Different types of fountain fills

Using Pattern Fills

You can fill objects with vector or bitmap pattern fills, as well as two-color fills. A two-color pattern fill is composed only of the two colors that you choose. A vector pattern fill is a more complex vector graphic composed of lines and fills. A vector fill can have color or transparent background. A bitmap pattern fill is a bitmap image whose complexity is determined by its size, image resolution, and bit depth.

To apply a two-color pattern fill, do this:

1. Select an object.

2. Click **Object** menu and choose **Object Properties**.

3. In the **Object properties** docker, click the **Fountain fill button** ▢ to display fountain fill options.

4. Choose a fill from the **Pattern Fill** picker from the list or create a custom pattern fill. For example, here to select the pattern from the list as shown in Figure 9.7.

5. Open the **Front color** picker, and click a color.

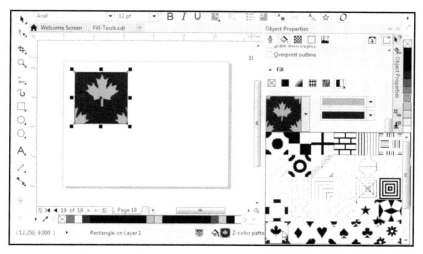

Figure 9.7 Applied two-colored pattern fill

6. Open the **Back color** picker, and click a color.

*You can also mix colors in a two-color pattern fill by pressing **Ctrl** and clicking a color on the color palette.*

To apply a vector or bitmap pattern fill, do this:

1. Select an object which you want to apply vector or bitmap pattern.

2. Click **Object** menu and choose **Object Properties**.

3. In the Fill area of the **Object properties** docker, click one of the following buttons.
   - Vector pattern fill
   - Bitmap pattern fill

4. Open the Fill picker, and click a pattern thumbnail as shown in Figure 9.8.

5. Click the **Apply** button ▣ in the pop-up window that appears.

To create a vector or bitmap pattern from an imported image, do this:

1. Select an object which you want to apply an imported image.

2. Click **Object** menu and choose **Object Properties**.

3. In the Fill area of the **Object properties** docker, click one of the following buttons.
   - Vector pattern fill
   - Bitmap pattern fill

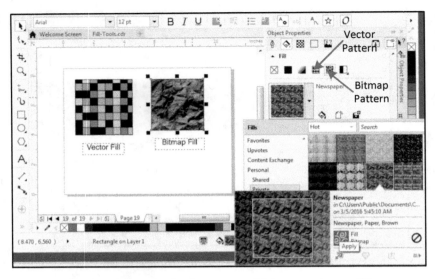

Figure 9.8   Applied vector and bitmap pattern fill

4. Click the **New source from file** button 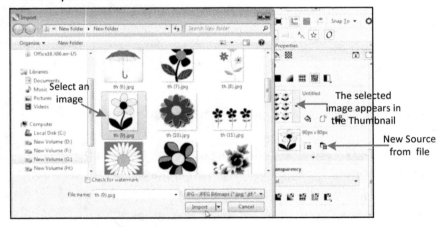.

5. The **Import** dialog box appears as shown in Figure 9.9. Locate the image that you want to use, and double-click the filename or click the **Import** button.

Figure 9.9   Select an image from Import dialog box to create vector or bitmap

6. The selected image in the bitmap thumbnail as shown in Figure 9.10.

If you want to modify a bitmap pattern fill do the following options:

7. In the Blend Transitions click the Mirror: tiles horizontally 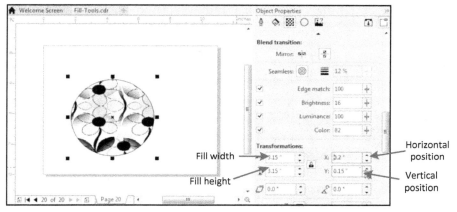 or the Mirror: tiles vertically button to arrange the tiles so that alternating tiles are vertical or horizontal reflections of each other. For example, here we select horizontally.

8. In the Seamless area, click the Radial button, or click the Linear button and move the slider. For example, here we have selected Radial blend a portion of the image diagonally in each pattern tile corner as shown in Figure 9.10.

Figure 9.10 Modified bitmap image pattern

This setting applies only to bitmap pattern fills.

9. Enable the **Edge match** check box, and move the slider, to smooth the color transition of the pattern tile edges with their opposite edge.

10. Enable the **Brightness** check box, and move the slider, to Increase or decrease the brightness of the pattern

11. Enable the **Luminance** check box, and move the slider, to Increase or decrease the grayscale contrast of the pattern.

12. Enable the **Color** check box, and move the slider, to Increase or decrease the color contrast of the pattern.

13. In the **Transformations**: area, type values in the Fill width and Fill

height boxes to set the width and height of the pattern as a percentage of the object's width and height.

14. Type values in the **X:** and **Y:** boxes to move the pattern horizontal position to center left or right, or move the pattern vertical position to center up or down.

The setting applied in the bitmap image options in the Object properties as shown in Figure 9.10.

To set row/column offset tile pattern, do this:

15. Click the **Row offset** ⠿ or the **Column offset** ⠿ button, and type a value in the **% of tile** box, to specify row or column offset as a percentage of the tile's height or width as shown in Figure 9.11.

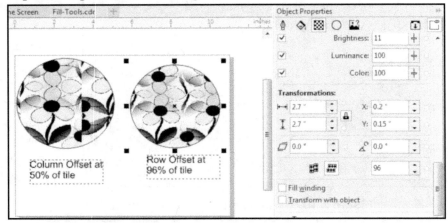

Figure 9.11 Set row/column offset tile pattern

If Rotate/Slant fill pattern at a specified angle, do the following options:

16. Type a value in the **Rotate** box, to rotate the pattern at a specified angle.

17. Type a value in the **Skew** box, to slant the pattern at a specified angle as shown in Figure 9.12.

Using Texture Fills

CorelDRAW X8 provides several preset textures for you to fill objects. Each texture has a set of attributes that can be changed as per your need. You can use existing texture fills, such as water, minerals, and clouds, or you can edit a texture to create your own texture fill.

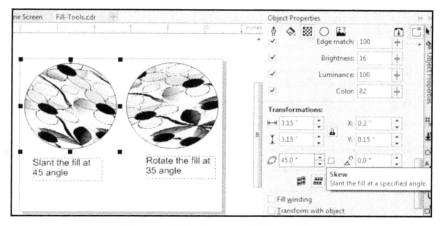

Figure 9.12 Skew and Slant fill pattern

To apply texture fills, do this:

1. Select an object.

2. Click **Object** menu and choose **Object Properties**.

3. In the **Fill** area of the **Object properties** docker, click the flyout arrow on the **Two-color pattern fill** button ◼️ and click the **Texture** fill button ▦ to display texture fill options.

4. Choose a texture library from the **Texture library**: list box.

5. Choose a texture from the **Texture list**: box. You can see the preview also as shown in Figure 9.13.

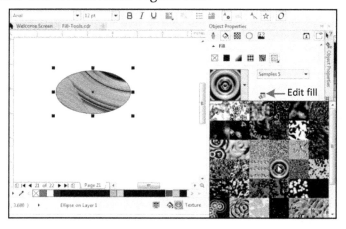

Figure 9.13 The Texture Fill dialog box

6. Click desired texture pattern you want to fill in the object.

To create a texture fill, do this:

1. Select an object.

2. Click **Object** menu and choose **Object Properties**.

3. In the **Fill** area of the **Object properties** docker, click the flyout arrow on the **Two-color pattern fill** button ▉ and click the **Texture fill** button ▦ to display texture fill options.

4. Choose a texture library from the **Texture Fill:** list box.

5. Choose a texture from the **Texture list:** box. You can see the preview also as shown in Figure 9.13.

6. Click the **Edit fill** ◈ button. The **Edit** dialog box appears as shown in Figure 9.14.

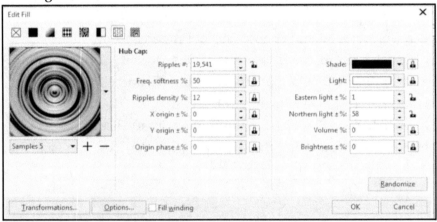

Figure 9.14 Edit Fill dialog box

7. Click the **Transformations…** button. The **Transformations** dialog box appears as shown in Figure 9.15.

8. In the **Blend transition:** area, click the **Mirror:** tiles horizontally ▦ or the **Mirror:** tiles vertically ▫ button to arrange the tiles so that alternating tiles are vertical or horizontal reflections of each other. For example, here we select horizontally.

9. Type a value in the **Fill width** and **Fill height** boxes to set the width and height to change the size of the fill.

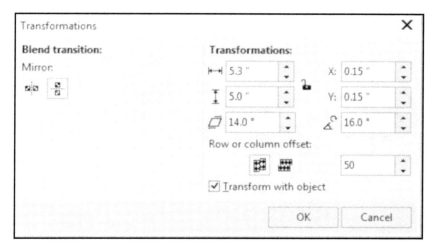

Figure 9.15 Set attributes in the Transformations dialog box to customize the texture

10. Type values in the **X:** and **Y:** boxes to move the pattern horizontal position to center left or right, or move the pattern vertical position to center up or down.

11. Click **Transformations, t**o rotate a texture fill, type a value in the **Rotate:** box.

12. Click **Transformations**, to skew a texture fill, type a value in the **Skew:** box. To applied a desired click OK button.

13. To offset the tile origin of a texture fill, enable the **Row** or **Column** option and type an amount of offset in the **% of tile size** box. To specify a row or column offset as a percentage of the tile's width or height. The difference in effect that occurs by choosing the different offsets is shown in Figure 9.16.

14. To further set the tiling options, click the **O̲ptions…** button. An **Options** dialog box appears as shown in Figure 9.17. Type a value in the **Bitmap resolution:** list box to specify the bitmap resolution to the texture fill. Set Maximum tile width you want in the **Maximum tile width** list box. To reset the default values for width and resolution, click on the **R̲eset** button and click Ok button.

15. To save a text, click the **Save texture** button in the property bar, and type a name in the **Texture name** box in the **Save texture as** dialog box. Choose a library from the **Library name** list box.

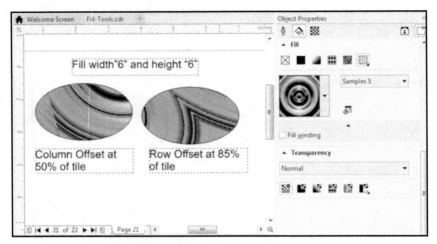

Figure 9.16 The effect of different offset of tiles

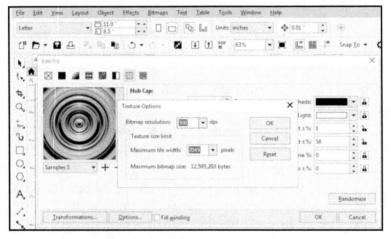

Figure 9.17 Texture Options dialog box

Using PostScript fills

PostScript texture fills are micro programs designed using PostScript language. You cannot customize PostScript fills as you do with other fill types. When you apply a PostScript texture fill, you can change several properties, such as the size, line width, and the amount of gray that appears in the texture's foreground and background.

To apply PostScript texture fills, do this:

1. Select the object to which you want to apply the fill.

2. Click Object menu and choose Object Properties.
3. In the Fill area of the Object properties docker, click the flyout arrow on the Two-color pattern fill button and click the PostScript fill button to display postscript fill options.
4. Choose a presets PostScript fill texture drop-down list and select desired postscript texture fill options as shown in Figure 9.18.

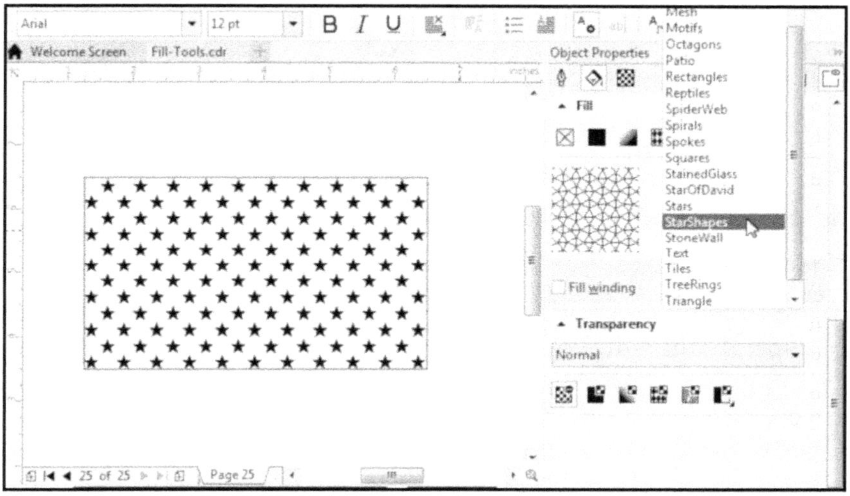

Figure 9.18 Selecting PostScript Texture

5. Click the Preview fill check box to see the preview of each of the texture (See Figure 9.18).
6. If you want to change the fill properties, click the Edit fill button and specify the settings you want.
7. The Edit fill dialog box appears as shown in Figure 9.19.
8. Specify parameters in the **Parameters**: area. Each PostScript texture has its own unique parameters. Some of the common parameters are Points, Frequency, Spacing, Angle and Gray.
9. After setting the new parameters, click the Refresh button to apply the new settings and click OK button.

You can also apply a PostScript fill by clicking the Interactive fill tool, clicking the PostScript fill button on the property bar, and choosing a fill from the PostScript fill textures list box.

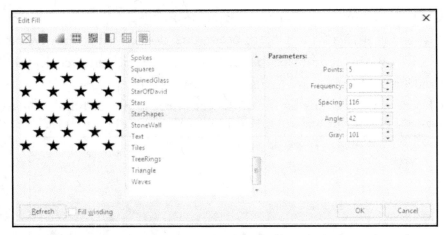

Figure 9.19 Change the postscript fill properties in Edit fill dialog box

Using Mesh fills

When you fill an object with a mesh fill, you can create unique effects. You can specify the number of columns and rows in the grid, and you specify the grid's intersecting points. After you have created a mesh object, you can edit the mesh fill grid by adding and removing nodes or intersections. You can also remove the mesh. In addition, you can smooth the color in a mesh fill to reduce the appearance of hard edges. You can also reveal objects underneath a selected area by applying transparency to the mesh fill.

To apply a mesh to an object, do this:

1. Select the object.

2. Click the Interactive fill flyout and choose the Interactive mesh fill tool.

3. In the property bar, type the number of columns and rows in the top and bottom portion of the Grid Size list box (See Figure 9.20).

4. Drag a color from the color palette to a patch in the object.

5. Make sure that the Smooth mesh color button on the property bar is enabled to reduce the appearance of hard edges in the mesh fill.

6. To add intersection, click at the point where you want to add the intersection and click the button on the property bar.

7. To delete any intersection, click on the intersection which you want to delete and click the button on the property bar.

8. You can also add a node or an intersection by double-clicking within a grid.

9. To delete a node, double click the node which you want to delete.

10. To shape the mesh fill, drag a new node to a new location (See Figure 9.20).

11. To remove the mesh fill, click the **Clear mesh** button on the property bar.

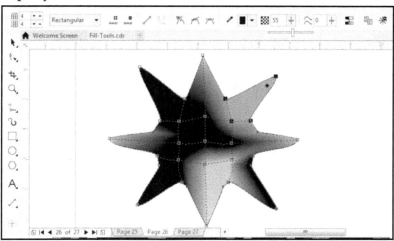

Figure 9.20 Changing the position and smooth and Transparency of mesh color fill

Changing the transparency of objects

When you apply a transparency to an object, you make the objects beneath it partially visible. You can apply transparencies by using the same kind of fills you apply to objects; that is, uniform, fountain, texture, and pattern.

To apply a uniform transparency, do this:

1. Select an object.

2. Click **Object** menu and choose **Object Properties**.

3. In the **Transparency** area of the **Object properties** docker, click the Uniform transparency button .

4. Move the **Transparency** slider to increase or decrease the transparency.

You can click a color on the color palette to apply a color to the transparency.

5. Select any of the transparency options

- **All**: Apply the transparency to both the object fill and the object outline.
- **Fill**: Apply the transparency only to the object fill, click the **Fill** 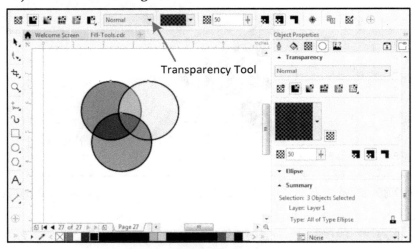 button.
- **Outline**: Apply the transparency only to the object outline. Click the Outline button.

6. For example, here we have selected the fill transparency to the object as shown in Figure 9.21.

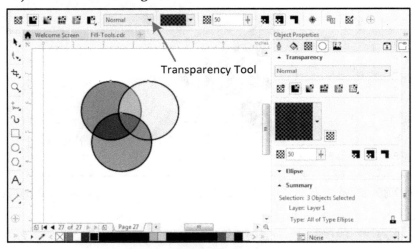

Figure 9.21 Applied uniform transparency fill

7. You can also click the **Transparency** tool in the toolbox and use the controls on the property bar.

Applying Fountain Transparency

Fountain transparency makes the object fade from one transparency value to another. The fountain transparency can be linear, elliptical, conical, or rectangular. You can create a fountain transparency by adding and removing nodes, and specifying a transparency value for each node. You can also reverse, mirror, resize, or skew a fountain transparency, or apply other transformations

1. Select an object.
2. Click **Object** menu and choose **Object Properties**.
3. In the **Transparency** area of the **Object properties** docker, click the **Fountain transparency** ![icon] button to display fountain transparency options.
4. Open the **Transparency** picker, and click a thumbnail.
5. Click the **Apply** button ![icon] in the pop-up window that appears as shown in Figure 9.22.

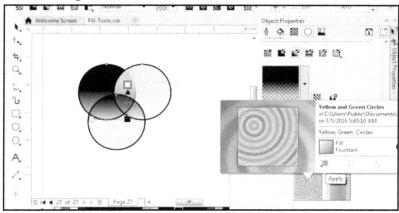

Figure 9.22 Fountain transparency applied to the object

To create a fountain transparency, do this:

1. Select an object.
2. Click **Object** menu and choose **Object Properties**.
3. In the **Transparency** area of the **Object properties** docker, click the **Fountain transparency** ![icon] button to display fountain transparency options.
4. Click one of the following buttons to choose a fountain transparency type:
   - **Linear fountain transparency** — It gradually changes opacity along a linear path.

- Elliptical fountain transparency—It gradually changes opacity in concentric ellipses from the center outwards.
- Conical fountain transparency— It gradually changes opacity in Conical shape.
- Rectangular fountain transparency— It gradually changes opacity in concentric rectangular from the center outwards.

5. Click the first node above the grayscale band, and type a value in the **Node transparency** box. For example, here we have type a Node transparency value at 9%.

6. Click the last node above the grayscale band, and type a value in the **Node transparency** box.

7. Select the midpoint node, and type a value in the **Node transparency** box to change the transparency of the midpoint.

8. To apply the transparency only to the Object Fill.

In Figure 9.23 and Figure 9.24 shows the three circles changes transparency in a linear, elliptical, conical and Elliptical fountain

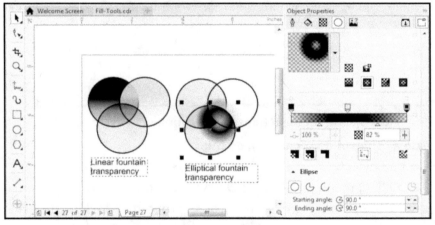

Figure 9.23 Linear and Elliptical fountain transparency

9. Click the **Edit transparency** button and click one of the following buttons
- Repeat and mirror
- Repeat
- Reverse transparency

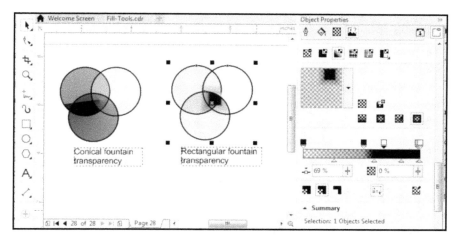

Figure 9.24 Conical and Rectangular fountain transparency

10. The **Edit Transparency** dialog box appears as shown in Figure 9.25 to choose the fill properties.

11. Click **Smooth** button to create smoother color transitions between fountain fill nodes.

In Figure 9.26, we have selected Rectangular fountain to **Reverse Transparency** to flip the transparency and move the **Acceleration** slider to quickly blends from one level of opacity to another. The changes applied in the object as shown in Figure 9.26.

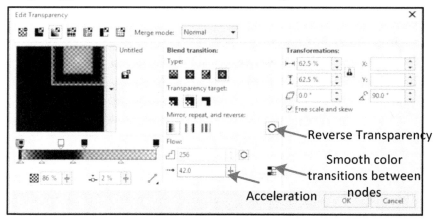

Figure 9.25 Change Properties in Edit Transparency dialog box

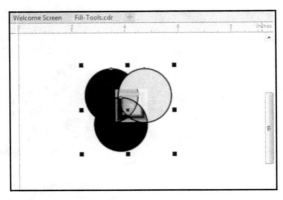

Figure 9.26 Reverse to flip transparency

You can also choose the following options:

1. Set the width and height of the transparency as a percentage of the object's width and height. Type values in the **Transparency width** and **Transparency height** boxes.

2. Type values in the **X** and **Y** boxes to move the transparency center up, down, left, or right.

3. Type a value in the **Skew** box to slant the transparency at a specified angle.

4. Type a value in the **Rotate** box to Rotate the transparency at a specified angle.

Applying Pattern Transparency

There are three types of pattern transparency:

Vector pattern transparency – this pattern composed of lines and fills, instead of dots of color like bitmaps.

Bitmap pattern transparency – this pattern composed of patterns of light and dark or differently colored pixels in a rectangular array.

Two-color pattern transparency – this pattern composed of "on" and "off" pixels.

CorelDRAW provides a collection of vector and bitmap patterns that you can access. Vector and bitmap patterns are made up of smaller units called tiles. Depending on the size of the object, the fill may consist of one or more tiles. You can create a new pattern by selecting an area of the workspace to use as a tile, or by using an imported image as a tile source.

To apply a vector or bitmap pattern transparency, do this:

1. Select an object which you want to apply an imported image.
2. Click Object menu and choose Object Properties.
3. In the Transparency area of the Object properties docker, click one of the following buttons.
   - Vector pattern transparency
   - Bitmap pattern transparency
4. Type values in the Foreground transparency and Background transparency boxes.
5. Click the Invert option to flip background and foreground transparency.
6. Select All to apply the transparency to both the object fill and the object outline.
7. The selected vector pattern transparency as shown in Figure 9.27.

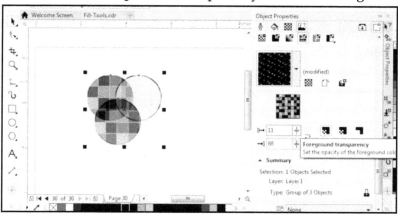

Figure 9.27 Applied vector pattern transparency

8. To modify the pattern, click the Edit transparency button, and specify the settings you want.

Applying Texture Transparency

You can use textures to create transparency effects. You can use existing textures, such as water, minerals, and clouds, or you can edit a texture to create your own texture transparency

To apply the texture transparency the same steps as you discussed in using texture fills.

Copying, Freezing, and Removing Transparencies

You can copy a transparency from one object to another. When you position a transparency over an object, you can freeze it, making the view of the object move with the transparency

To copy a transparency from another object, do this:

1. In the toolbox, click the Transparency tool ⊞ buton.

2. Select the object to which you want to copy the transparency as shown in Figure 9.28.

3. Click the **Copy transparency** button ⊞ on the property bar.

4. Click the object from which you want to copy the transparency.

5. The object gets the same transparency to be copied the selected object transparency as shown in Figure 9.29.

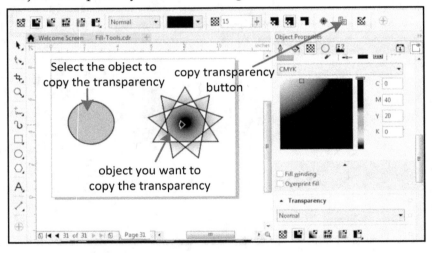

Figure 9.28 Select the object to copy the transparency

To freeze the contents of a transparency, do this:

1. In the toolbox, click the Transparency tool ⊞ buton.

2. Select an object to which a transparency has been applied.

3. Click the **Freeze transparency** ✳ button on the property bar as shown in Figure 9.30.

To remove a transparency, do this:

1. Select an object to which a transparency has been removed.

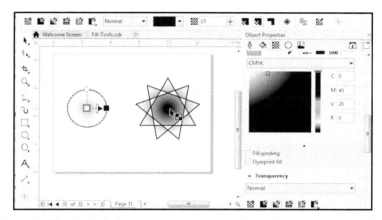

Figure 9.29 Copied the transparency to selected transparency object

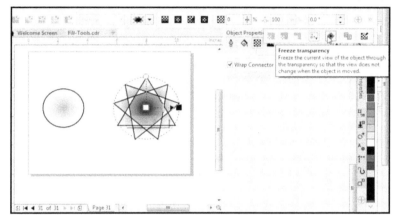

Figure 9.30 Freeze transparency

2. In the Transparency area of the Object properties docker, click the No transparency button.

CHAPTER 10

Special Effects to Objects

Introduction

In this chapter, you will learn applying special effects to object. It means using applying Lenses contain creative effects that let you change the appearance of an object without actually changing the object. Lenses change how the object area beneath the lens appears, not the actual properties and attributes of the objects. You can apply lenses to any vector object, such as a rectangle, ellipse, closed path, or polygon. You can also change the appearance of artistic text and bitmaps.

Adding 3D effects to objects which create the illusion of three-dimensional (3D) depth in objects by adding contour, perspective, extrusion, bevel, or drop shadow effects. All these tools are available in the Interactive Fill Tool flyout as shown in Figure 10.1. You will learn how to use these interactive tools.

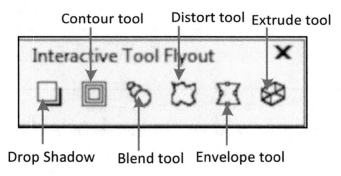

Figure 10.1 The Interactive Tool flyout

To apply a lens, do this:

1. Select an object. For example, we have create a small star and make it group.

2. Draw Ellipses over the Star object.

3. Click Effects menu and choose Lens. Alternatively press Alt+F3 keys together. The Lens docker window appears.

4. Choose a lens type from the list box in the **Lens** docker window. For example, we have selected **Fish eye** lens. It creates the effect of distort, magnify, or shrink the objects beneath the lens. (See Figure 10.2).

5. In the **Rate**: list box specify the percentage value. For example, we have set the value at 140%.

6. Click **Apply** button.

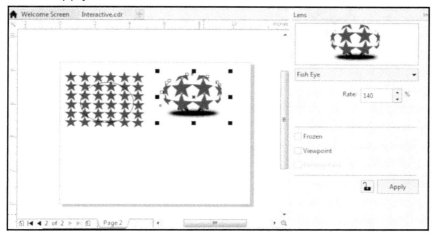

Figure 10.2 Fish eye lens effect applied in the vector image

Creating Drop Shadows

Drop shadows simulate light falling on an object from one of five particular perspectives: flat, right, left, bottom, and top. When you add a drop shadow, you can change its perspective, and you can adjust attributes such as color, opacity, fade level, angle, and feathering.

To add a drop shadow, do this:

1. In the toolbox, click the **Drop shadow** ⬚ tool.

2. Click an object as shown in Figure 10.3.

3. Drag from the center or side of the object until the drop shadow is the size you want.

4. Specify the attributes on the property bar as shown in Figure 10.4.

   • **Preset List**: To set the drop shadow option.

   • **Drop Shadow Angle**: To set the direction of the drop shadow.

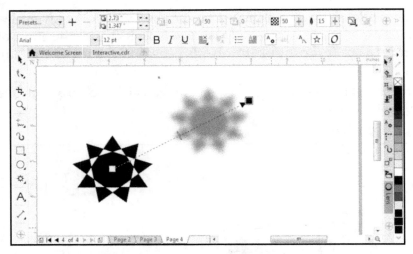

Figure 10.3 Add a Drop shadow into the object

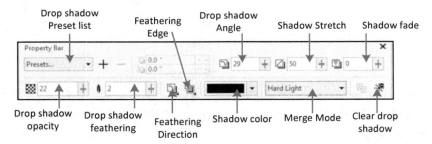

Figure 10.4 Drop shadow property bar

- **Shadow Stretch**: To adjust the length of the drop shadow.
- **Shadow Fade**: To adjust the amount of fading at the edges of the drop shadow.
- **Drop shadow Opacity**: To adjust the transparency of the drop shadow.
- **Shadow Feathering**: To sharpen or soften edges of the drop shadow.
- **Feathering Direction**: To soften the shadows edges toward the inside of the shadow, toward the outside of the shadow or both of the direction.
- **Feather Edge**: To choose the feathering type.

- **Shadow color**: To apply color of the drop shadow.
- **Merge mode**: Choose the color of the drop shadow blends with the color of the underlying object as shown in Figure 10.5.

5. To choose the above desired setting you want to apply drop shadow for the object.

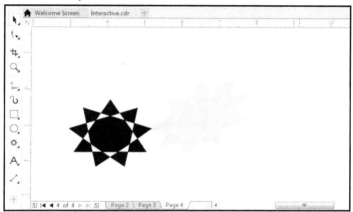

Figure 10.5 Drop shadow angle at the direction to 20 degree from Flat Top Right preset option

To remove a drop shadow, do this:

1. Select an object's drop shadow.
2. Click **Effects** menu and choose **Clear drop shadow**.
   - You can also remove a drop shadow from an object by clicking the **Clear drop shadow** button on the property bar.

Contouring objects

You can contour an object to create a series of concentric lines that progress to the inside or outside of the object. It also lets you set the number and distance of the contour lines.

You can also choose how contour corners appear. For example, you can use pointed or rounded corners, or you can bevel (square off) sharp contour corners. You can separate an object from its contour lines.

To contour an object, do this:

1. In the toolbox, click the **Contour** tool as shown in Figure 10.6.

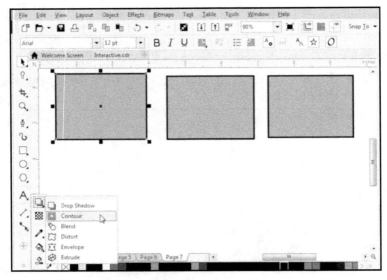

Figure 10.6 Select the Object with Contour tool

2. Click an object or a set of grouped objects, and drag the start handle toward the center to create an inside contour or away from the center to create an outside contour.

3. Move the object slider to change the number of contour steps.

4. Specify the desired options on the property bar as shown in Figure 10.7 to apply the contouring to an object.

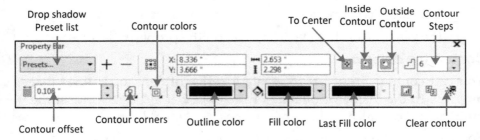

Figure 10.7 Contour Property Bar

- Add contour lines to the center of the selected object, to click the **To center** button.

- Click the **Inside contour** or **Outside contour** button on the property bar, and type a value in the **Contour steps** box on the property bar.

- Type a value in the **Contour offset** box on the property bar, to specify the distance between contour lines.

5. Click the corner triangle to select the type of contour corners in the property bar.

- Click the **Mitered corners** button, to use pointed contour corners.

- Click the **Round corners** button, to use rounded contour corners.

- Click the **Bevel corners** button, to use beveled contour corners.

6. To choose the above desired setting you want to apply contour effect for the object as shown in Figure 10.8. For example, here we have set the preset option as Inward and different types of contour corners to the rectangle object.

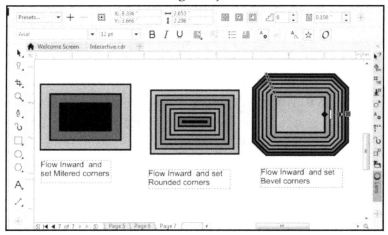

Figure 10.8 Inward preset option and different types of corners

You can create contours by clicking **Effects** menu and **Contour** and specifying the settings you want in the Contour docker.

To separate an object from its contour lines, do this:

1. Select a contoured object using the **Pick** tool.

2. Click the **Object** menu and choose **Break Contour Group Apart** as shown in Figure 10.9. Alternatively, press **Ctrl+K** keys together.

3. The contour lines get separated from the object as shown in Figure 10.9.

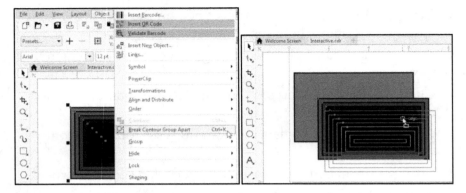

Figure 10.9 Selecting Break Contour Group apart from object menu and the lines get separated from the rectangle

Applying perspective to objects

You can create a perspective effect by shortening one or two sides of an object. This effect gives an object the appearance of receding in one or two directions, thereby creating a one-point perspective or a two-point perspective.

To apply a two-point perspective, do this:

1. Select an object to which you want to apply a perspective effect.
2. Click **Effects** menu and choose **Add Perspective**... .
3. Drag the nodes on the outside of the grid to apply the effect you want as shown in Figure 10.10.

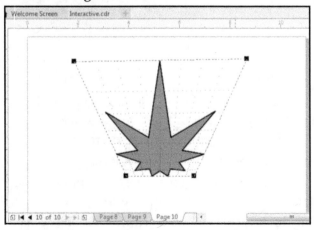

Figure 10.10   Applied two-point perspectives to the Object

To remove a perspective effect from an object, do this:

1. Select an object that has a perspective effect.

2. Click Effe̲cts menu and choose Clea̲r Perspective...

Blending Objects

Blending one object to another means, filling the space between the two objects with intermediary objects. CorelDRAW X8 lets you blend one object to another. These intermediary objects illustrate a step-by-step transition from the first object to the second object. The transition is not only in size and shape but in color also. You can also define a path for the blend.

To blend an object into another, do this:

1. Click the Blend Tool from the toolbox.

2. Click the first object and drag to the second object. When you release the mouse, you will observe intermediate objects connecting the three objects. Figure 10.11 shows a star blended into an circle.

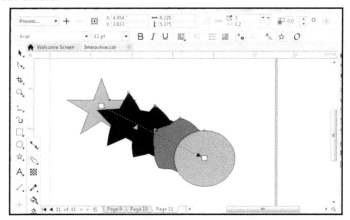

Figure 10.11   The star have been blended into a circle with three intermediate steps

3. In the Property bar, change the number of steps or adjust the spacing between steps in the Blend objects list box, fixes the number of steps you want in between the two objects.

4. You can blend an object along a freehand path, hold down Alt, key and drag to draw a line to the second object.

5. To blend along a predefined path, draw a curve (the path). Then click on the **Path Properties** button and choose **New Path**. (See Figure 10.12)

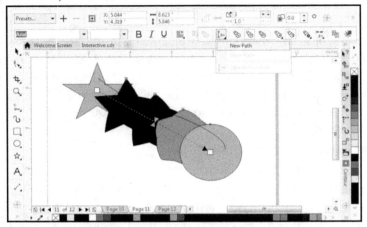

Figure 10.12   Pointing to tohe curve that will define the path for the blen

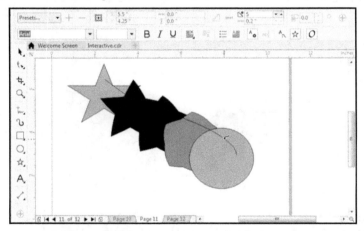

Figure 10.13   The blend follows the path of the curve

6. Now, point to the curve as shown in Figure 10.13.
7. You will observe that the original objects and the intermediary objects align themselves on the curve (See Figure 10.13).
8. Stretch the blend over an entire path, select a blend that has already fitted on a path. Click the **More blend options** button

on the property bar, and enable the **Blend along full path** check box as shown in Figure 10.14.

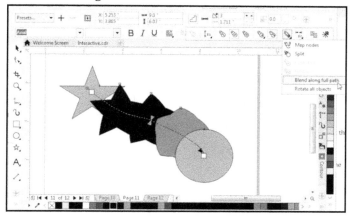

Figure 10.14   Selecting Stretch the blend over an entire path

☞ *If you change the size, shape, color or any other characteristics of the original objects, the characteristics of the intermediate objects will change automatically.*

To set the distance between objects in a blend that is, fit to a path do this:

1. Select a blend that is fit to a path.
2. Click the **Blend spacing** button ⊢⊣ on the property bar.
3. Type a value in the **Blend objects** box on the property bar as shown in Figure 10.15.
4. Press Enter.

☞ *If you have used the Blend along full path command, the Blend spacing button is unavailable*

To split a blend, do this:

1. Select a blend.
2. Click the **More blend options** button 🌀 on the property bar.
3. Click the **Split** 🌀 button.
4. Click the intermediate object at the point at where you want to split the blend.

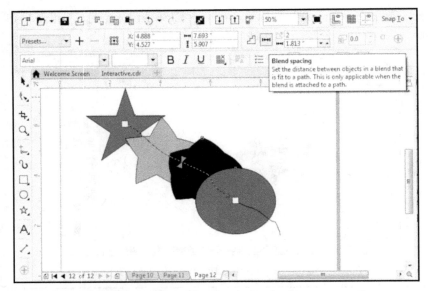

Figure 10.15   Select Blend spacing in the property bar

To remove a blend, do this:

1. Select a blend

2. Click **Effe̲cts** menu and choose **Clear blends**.

Distorting Objects

The distortion tool lets you apply a *Push* or *Pull* distortion, a *Zipper* distortion, or *a Twister distortion* to an object.

- The Push or Pull Distortion lets you push the edges of an object in or pull the edges out of the object.

- The Zipper distortion lets you apply a saw tooth like edge to the object. You can adjust the amplitude and frequency of the effect.

- The Twister distortion twists the object. The direction and degree of twist can be adjusted according to your will.

Figure 10.16 shows the effect of applying these three distortions on a rectangle.

To distort an object, do this:

1. Select the object, which is to be distorted.

2. Click the **Interactive Tool** flyout and choose the **Distort Tool**.

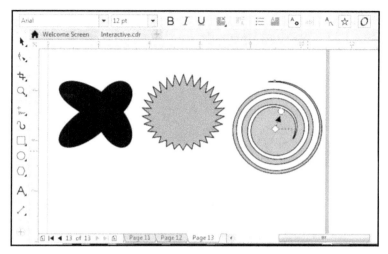

Figure 10.16   Effect of different distort on a circle

3. In the property bar, one of the following buttons, and specify the settings you want.

Push and Pull Distortion

1. Draw a rectangle object.

2. In the Property bar, click the **Push and Pull Distortion** button have shown in Figure 10.17.

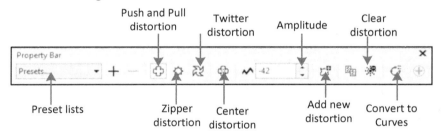

Figure 10.17   Push and Pull Property bar options

3. You can select a preset distortion from the **Preset** drop down list. You can select the pull or push corners as shown in Figure 10.18.

4. *Alternatively*, click on the object where you want the centre of distortion to be placed.

5. Without releasing mouse, drag until the object is of the shape you wanted.

6. You will observe a diamond shaped position handle (when the object is clicked once) at the centre of distortion (See Figure 10.18).

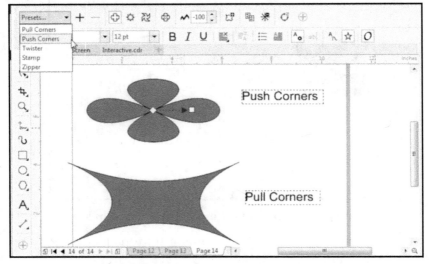

Figure 10.18   Pull and push Distortion Corners

Copy Distortion

1. Select the object to which you want to copy a distortion.
2. Click Eff**e**cts menu choose Cop**y** Effect and select **D**istortion From... .
3. Click a distorted object.
4. *Alternatively,* you can use the Eyedropper tool to copy the effect.

Zipper Distortion

1. Draw a circle in the drawing window.
2. Click the **Zipper Distortion** button in the property bar. The Property bar for Zipper distortion has shown in Figure 10.19.
3. You can choose from preset zipper distortion listed in the **Preset List:** list box.
4. Specify the amplitude of the distortion in the **Zipper Amplitude** list box to adjust the height of the teeth in the sawtooth effect.
5. Specify the frequency of the distortion in the **Zipper frequency** list box to adjust the number of teeth in the sawtooth effect.

6. *Alternatively,* drag the nodes of the object to apply a zipper distortion of your choice to the object.

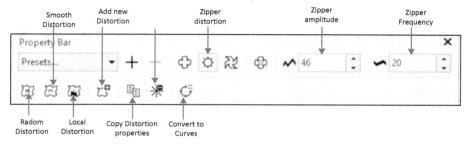

Figure 10.19   Zipper property bar options

7. Select any of the distortion effects such as

   Randomize distortion: Randomize the effects of the distortion.

   Smooth distortion: Smooth the nodes in the distortion.

   Localize distortion: To reduce the effects of the distortion as it progresses.

8. For example, here we have different effect of distortion in the circle object as shown in Figure 10.20.

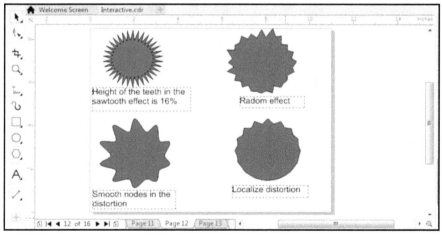

Figure 10.20   Different types of distortion effects

Twister Distortion

1. Click the **Twister Distortion** button. The property bar for Twister distortion has shown in Figure 10.21.

2. You can choose from preset twister distortions given in the **Preset** list box.

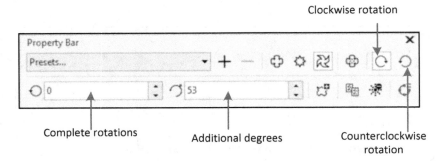

Figure 10.21   Twister property bar options

3. Specify the direction of twist by clicking on the **Clockwise Rotation** or **Counterclockwise Rotation** button.

4. Now specify the number of twists in the **Complete Rotations** list box.

5. Specify angle of twist in the **Additional Degrees** list box.

6. *Alternatively,* drag the nodes of the object, until the distortion is of the shape you desire. For example, here we have selected Additional degrees set at 61% to complete rotation for the distortion as shown in Figure 10.22.

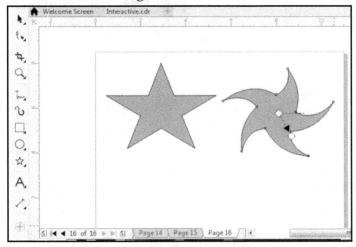

Figure 10.22   Twister distortion at additional degrees set at 61 percentage

Extruding Objects

You can add a 3-D effect to an object using the **Interactive Extrude Tool**. Extrusion combines 3-D effects with shadows and the object inherits a three dimensional look. You can create vector extrusions by projecting points from an object and joining them to create an illusion of three dimensions. CorelDRAW X8 also lets you apply a vector extrusion to an object in a group. You can change an extruded form by rotating it and rounding its corners.

To extrude an object, do this:

1. Select the object, which is to be extruded.
2. Click the **Interactive** flyout and choose **Extrude Tool**. The property bar provides a wide variety of options for extrusion. The Extrude options available in property bar are explain in Figure 10.23.

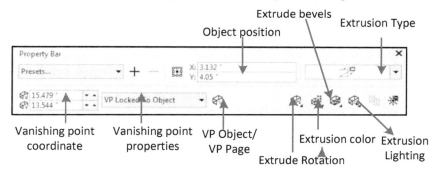

Figure 10.23   The Interactive Extrude property bar

3. You can choose from a list of predefined extrusions options available in the **Preset** list box. For example, select Top Right.
4. Drag the object's selection handles to set the direction and depth of the extrusion. Figure 10.24 shows the object being extruded in Top right direction.
5. You can also specify object's horizontal and vertical position in the x: and y: box respectively. Experiment with other options available in the Property bar and observe the effects for yourself.
6. Select the **Extrusion type**, from the drop down list.
7. To rotate an extrusion, select an extruded object. Click the **Extrude** rotation button on the property bar. Drag the extrusion in the direction you want.

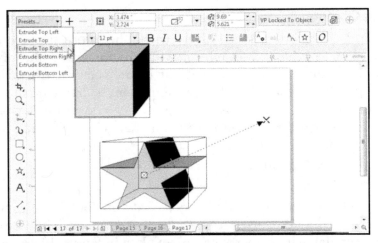

Figure 10.24   Selecting Extrude Top right options from the preset list

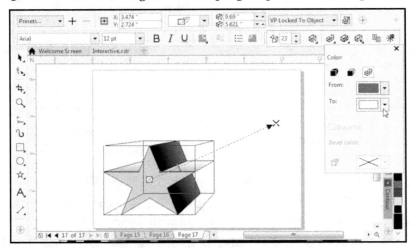

Figure 10.25   Choosing color and shading extrusion effect

8. Click the **Color** button and choose a color for selected object. You also have the option of bringing the extrusion effect using color shading. If you choose **Use Color Shading**, specify a color in the From: and To: drop down color palette (See Figure 10.25). In our case, the extrusion effect starts from the color you choose in the From: list and ends in the color you choose in the To: list.

9. Select an extruded object. Click the **Bevels** button on the property

bar. Enable the **Use bevel** check box. Type a value in the **Bevel Depth** box and **Bevel Angle** box as seen in Figure 10.26.

10. You can also set the bevel depth and angle by using the **Interactive display** box in the bevel list box. You can show only the bevel and hide the extrusion by enabling the **Show Bevel Only** check box. (See Figure 10.26)

11. To add some lighting to the object, click the **Lighting** button and choose a light number and intensity. The effect on the object is felt accordingly.

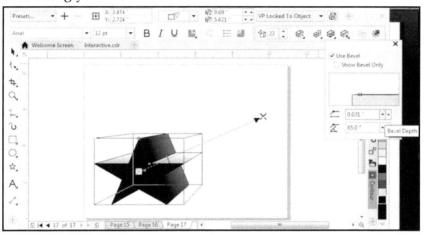

Figure 10.26   Select Use Bevel options

12. To copy **Extrude properties** to another object, do the following:

- Select the object you want to extrude.

- Click the **Effects** menu and choose either **Copy Effect** or **Clone Effect**. Select the **Extrude From…** you will see the black arrow. Click the extruded object, then you will feel the effect of the object.

13. To remove a vector extrusion Click the **Clear extrude** button on the property bar.

Interactive Envelopes

You can confine objects in frames called envelopes. When nodes of these envelopes are dragged, the objects contained within them, change shapes accordingly. You can apply four types of envelopes to an object – *Straight Line, Single Arc, Double Arc* and *Unconstrained* Envelopes. These envelopes are shown in Figure 10.27.

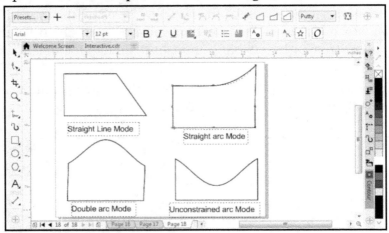

Figure 10.27   Effect of dragging (in same direction and amount) on different envelope types

- *Straight Line envelopes* are based on straight lines adding perspective to objects.
- *Single Arc envelopes* have an arc shape on one side, giving objects the concave or convex appearance.
- *Double Arc envelopes* have an S shape on one or more sides.
- *Unconstrained envelopes* are freeform envelopes that allow adding, changing and deleting nodes.

To apply envelope to an object, do this:

1. Select the object. Or create an artistic text by applying envelopes to them.

2. Click the **Interactive** flyout and choose **Envelope Tool.**

3. In the property bar, click on **Envelope Straight line mode, Envelope Single arc Mode, Envelope Double arc Mode** or **Envelope Unconstrained Mode** button, depending on which type of envelope you need. Figure 10.28 shows the property bar for the **Envelope Tool** options.

4. Drag Pull or push the nodes of the envelope until the object is of the shape you desire.

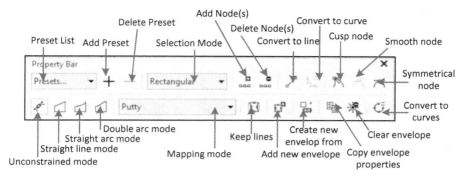

Figure 10.28   Envelope property bar options

5. You can also apply a preset envelope to an object by choosing one from the **Preset** list box as shown in Figure 10.29.

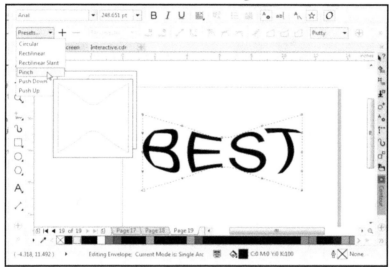

Figure 10.29   The "BEST" text has been modified inside an envelope

6. To add envelope to an object that is already enveloped, click on the **Add New Envelope** button.

7. To remove envelope, click **Effects** menu and choose **Clear Envelope.**

8. To keep the straight lines of objects straight, click on the **Keep Lines** button.

Free Transformations

You can *rotate, skew, scale, stretch* and *position* an object interactively using the Transformation Docker window. By skewing an object, we mean distorting the object shape non-proportionally. Scaling means changes made in horizontal or vertical dimensions of an object.

To open the Transformations docker window, do this:

1. Click <u>W</u>indows menu, highlight <u>D</u>ockers, highlight <u>T</u>ransformations and choose any of the options available.

2. The Transformation Docker window appears as shown in Figure 10.30.

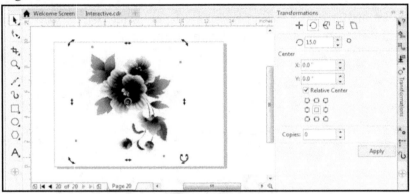

Figure 10.30   Figure rotated through the Rotate Transformation docker window

To rotate an object, do this:

1. Select the object, which is to be rotated.

2. In the docker window click the **Rotate** button (See Figure 10.30).

3. Click any of the checkboxes below the **Relative Center** check box, specify the position around which the object is to be rotated.

4. Type the angle through which the object is to be rotated in the **Angle of rotation** list box.

5. Specify the horizontal and vertical coordinates around which you want to rotate the object in the **X:** and **Y:** list box respectively.

6. Click **Apply**.

To scale an object, do this:

1. Select the object

2. Click the **Scale and Mirror** button (See Figure 10.31).

3. In the **X** and **Y** list boxes, specify the percentage by which you want to scale horizontally and vertically the object.

4. Click on the **Horizontal Mirror** button to flip the object horizontally i.e. left to right and vice versa.

5. Click on the **Vertical Mirror** button to flip the object vertically i.e. top to bottom and vice versa.

6. Click **Apply**.

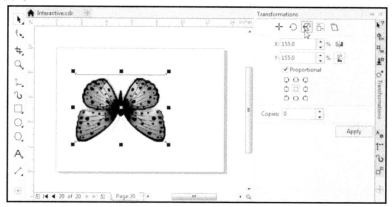

Figure 10.31   Figure scaled and flipped horizontally.

To size the object, do this:

1. Select the object.

2. Click on the **Size** button (See Figure 10.32).

3. To stretch the object disproportionably, enable the **Non-proportional** check box otherwise disable it.

4. Specify the new width and height of the object in the **X** and **Y** boxes respectively.

5. Click **Apply**.

To skew an object, do this:

1. Select the object, which is to be skewed.

2. Click the **Skew** button (See Figure 10.33).

3. Specify the number of degrees by which you want to skew the object horizontally and vertically in the **X** and **Y** list boxes respectively.

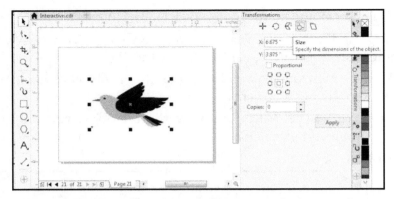

Figure 10.32   The Size Transformations docker window

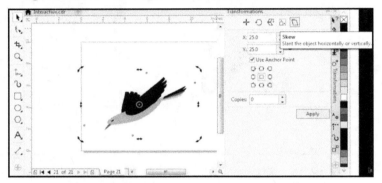

Figure 10.33   Slant the object at 25 degree

4. Click Apply.

To position an object in a new location, do this:

1. Select the object.

2. Click on the Positions button.

3. Disable the Relative position check box.

4. Specify the horizontal and vertical position of the object in the X and Y boxes respectively.

5. Click Apply.

    To close the docker window, click the close button on the window. When you select an object with pick tool, the transformation features are available in the property bar. You can apply rotation, skewing, scaling and sizing transformations to the object through this property bar.

CHAPTER 11

Working with Images

Introduction

In this Chapter, you will learn to import and export an image, as well as how to modify or manipulate them. You must have got an idea by now that CorelDRAW X8 works fine with Vector images. But CorelDRAW X8 is also capable of working on bitmap images, wherein the images are created in the form of dots, better known as pixels. In addition, CorelDRAW X8 comes packaged with Corel PHOTO-PAINT, a powerful program for creating and editing bitmap images.

Image Formats

You may have read about various image formats like *GIF, JPG, TIFF, EPS,* etc. An image format defines how application package stores information in a file. CorelDRAW X8 images are stored in *CDR* format and Bitmap images are stored in *BMP* format. The image format is identified by the three-letter extension appended at the end of a filename. This filename extension helps you to identify the type of file. The computer also differentiates among different types of files or file formats using the extensions.

If you want to use an image created in a different application package, then you need to import that file to be read by your package. Similarly, if you created an image in CorelDRAW X8, but you want to use it in another application, you must export the file to a different file format readable by that package.

Importing Files

You can import files created in other applications. For example, you can import an Adobe Portable Document Format (PDF), JPEG, or Adobe Illustrator (AI) file. You can import a file and place it in the active application window as an object. You can also resize and center a file as you import it.

To import an image, do this:

1. Click File menu and choose Import... .

2. In the **Import** dialog box, choose the folder where the file is stored from the **Address bar** (See Figure 11.1).

3. If you don't know the file's format, choose **All file formats.**

4. The file appears in the content pane. Select the desired file to import in the drawing window.

5. The file name with extensions appears in the **File name:** drop-down list.

Figure 11.1 The Import dialog box

6. Click **Import**, and do one of the following:

   • Click the drawing page to maintain the dimensions of the file and position its top-left corner where you click.

   • Drag on the drawing page to resize the file. The import cursor displays the dimensions of the resized file as you drag on the drawing page.

   • Press Enter to center the file on the drawing page.

   • Press the Spacebar to place the file in the same position as it was in the original file (CDR and AI files only).

7. Select the desired options where you want to place the image and click. Image will be placed at this location.

Bitmap Images

Bitmap images are images defined in the form of small dots called pixels. Unlike vector images, these are not defined interms of curves and lines. There are two main properties of bitmap images. These are:

- Resolution
- Number of colors in the image.

The resolution is expressed in dots per inch (dpi). For a computer monitor, 72 (dpi) dots per square inch is ideal but for printing purposes 600 or 1200 dpi is widely used. You can import bitmap images in the same way as you import other image formats. You can also convert any of the images into a bitmap image.

To convert an image into bitmap image, do this:

1. Select the image which is to be converted.
2. Click <u>B</u>itmaps menu and choose **Convert to Bitmap**... .
3. The **Convert To Bitmap** dialog box appears as shown in Figure 11.2.

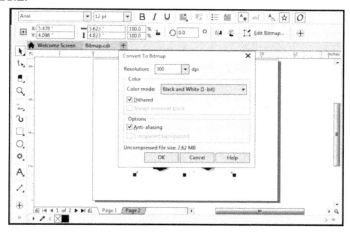

Figure 11.2 Convert to Bitmap dialog box

4. In the dialog box, choose a color mode from the **Color mode**: drop down menu. For example, here we have chosen Black and White (1-bit) as shown in Figure 11.2.
5. Specify a resolution of your choice in the **Resolution**: list box.
6. Click <u>A</u>nti-aliasing check box to smooths the edges of the bitmap.
7. To eliminate any colored background in the image, check the <u>T</u>ransparent Background check box.
8. Click OK. In Figure 11.3 shows the black and white (1-bit) color mode.

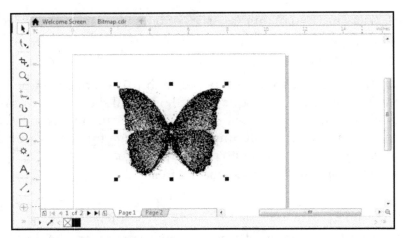

Figure 11.3 Black and white color mode

Cropping Bitmap Image

Cropping a bitmap image means cutting it short. In other words cropping an image means trimming an image.

To crop a bitmap image, do this:

1. Select the image
2. Click **Shape** flyout and choose **Shape Tool**.
3. Drag inwards the nodes of the image in which direction you want to crop (See Figure 11.4).

   If you want to add a node, double-click the node boundary (dotted line) by using the **Shape** tool where you want the node to appear.

4. Click **B̲itmaps** menu and choose **Crop bitmap**.

Bitmap Special Effects

You can apply a range of useful effects to bitmap images. These effects are Color masking i.e. removing a selected color from the image, transforming color, applying contour, etc. Most of these effects are available in the Bitmap menu. Some of them are explained here.

To apply 3D effects, do this:

1. Select the image.
2. Click **B̲itmaps** menu, highlight **3̲D Effects** and choose the effect that you want to apply (See Figure 11.5).

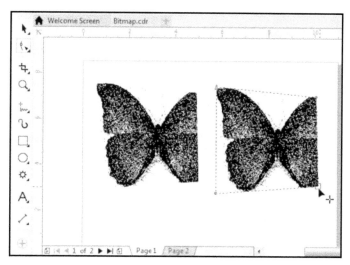

Figure 11.4 Node dragged in with the shape tool (left). Image after being cropped (right)

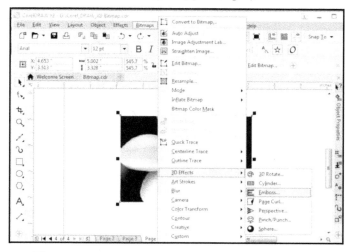

Figure 11.5 Select 3D Effects for Bitmap Images

3. Here, we have choose **Emboss**... . **Emboss** dialog box appears as shown in Figure 11.6.

4. Slide the **Depth**: and the **Level**: slider to specify the emboss depth and level.

5. Also specify the angle at which light hits the engraving in the **Direction**: list box.

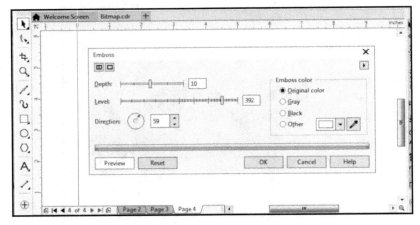

Figure 11.6 The Emboss dialog box

Figure 11.7 Embossed Image

6. Choose an embossing color from the **Emboss color** area. Use the eyedropper button to select a color from outside the dialog box.

7. Click the preview button to preview the image.

8. Click **OK** button to see the illusion effect as shown in Figure 11.7.

To apply Art Strokes, do this:

1. Select the image.

2. Click **Bitmaps** menu, highlight **Art Strokes** and choose from any of the available strokes as shown in Figure 11.8.

3. Here, we have choose P<u>a</u>stels… . The **Pastels** dialog box appears as shown in Figure 11.9.

4. In the **Pastels Type** area, choose <u>S</u>oft for a soft pastel or choose <u>O</u>il for a smudged pastel.

5. Drag the slider of the **Stroke size**: to set the size of brushstroke.

6. Set the color variations of brushstrokes in the **Hue Variation**: area.

7. Click the preview button to preview the image.

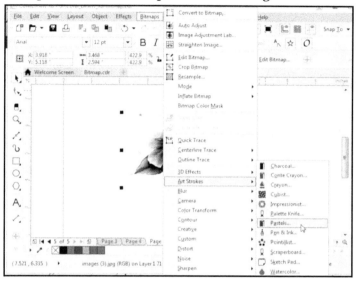

Figure 11.8 Art stroke Effects for Bitmap images

Figure 11.9 Pastels dialog box

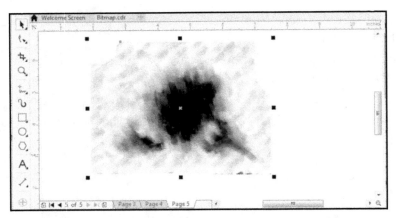

Figure 11.10 An Oil Pastel stroke applied to the image

8. Click OK to see the effect of the image (See Figure 11.10).

You will observe two small buttons on the top left corner of the Pastel dialog box. These buttons are seen in almost all the effects dialog box. Clicking on the first button will show the before and after applying effect preview of the image. The second image shows the effect in a single preview window. At the top right corner of each of the Effect dialog box, there is a small triangle. Clicking on it will show all the effects available in Bitmaps menu in a drop down menu.

To transform color, do this:

1. Select the image.
2. Click Bitmaps menu, highlight Color Transform and choose from any of the available options as shown in Figure 11.11.

Figure 11.11 The different Color Transform options

3. As an example, choose **S̲olarize**.... The **Solarize** dialog box appears as shown in Figure 11.12.

4. Drag the Slider to set the **Level:** by using color reduction. Click OK. A **Solarize Color Transform** applied to the image as shown in Figure 11.13.

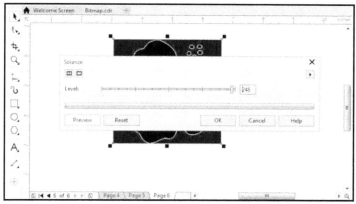

Figure 11.12   Solarize dialog box

Figure 11.13   Solarize color transform applied to an image

To distort images, do this:

1. Select the image.

2. Click **B̲itmaps** menu, highlight **D̲istort** and choose from any of the available options.

3. Here, we have choose **Swi̲rl**... . The **Swirl** dialog box appears as shown in Figure 11.14.

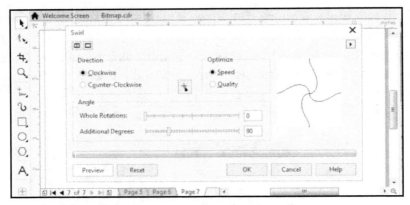

Figure 11.14 Setting attributes in the Swirl dialog box

4. Select any one of the radio button, **C**lockwise or **C**ounter-**Clockwise** direction in which the image gets twist.

5. In the **Angle** area, move the **Whole Rotations:** slider to increase and decrease or type a value in the Whole Rotations box to rotate the image.

6. Move the slider, at the right corner of the box to increase or decrease the angle of the **A**dditional **Degrees:** select the fixed degree, to fix the image.

7. Click OK. The distort effect applied in an image as shown in Figure 11.15.

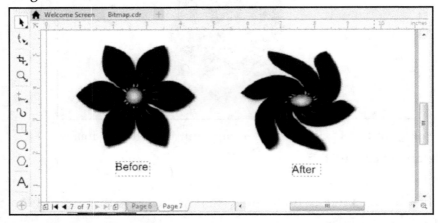

Figure 11.15 Image of the flower (right) has been converted into a twist form

To add noise, do this:

1. Select the image.
2. Click **B**itmaps menu, highlight **N**oise and choose **A**dd Noise. Add Noise dialog box appears as shown in Figure 11.16.
3. Specify noise type in the **Noise type** area.

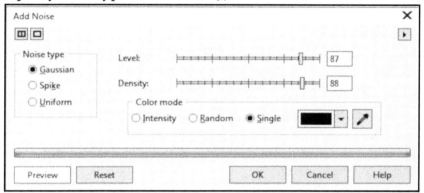

Figure 11.16   The Add Noise Dialog box

4. Specify level and density by dragging the **Level:** and **Density:** slider respectively.
5. Click **OK**.
6. Choose a color mode from the **Color mode** area. Select **S**ingle mode radio button to applied single color graininess effect in an image as shown in Figure 11.17.

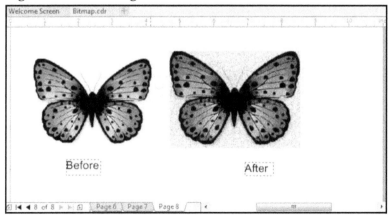

Figure 11.17   The Image on the Right Side has Added Noise to it

There are many other effects available for Bitmap images. You can experiment with other effects.

Color Masking

Color masking removes pixels having a selected color.

To apply color mask to a bitmap image, do this:

1. Select the image.
2. Click **Bitmaps** menu and choose **Bitmap Color Mask**. The **Bitmap Color Mask** docker window appears as shown in Figure 11.18.
3. Click on the **Hide Color** option on the docker window.
4. Slide the **Tolerance** slider to specify the exactness of the color to be removed.
5. Now, click the **Eyedropper** icon and click on the color in the image which is to be removed.

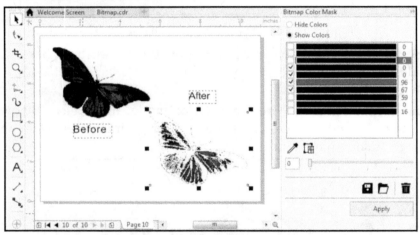

Figure 11.18 The Color Mask docker window. Observe that the inside color of the tree has been removed from the figure

6. You will observe that the chosen color appears in the first bar of the Bitmap Color Mask rollup.
7. When the color in the rollup matches the color you want to delete, and then click **Apply**. Watch that color and any other similar colored pixels (depending on the Tolerance) disappear.

8. If you need to delete additional colors from bitmap image, use the remaining bars in the Bitmap Color Mask rollup. But before you click Apply, disable the check boxes next to the color which you do not want to remove.

9. To reset the previous color of the image, click on the Remove Mask button.

Resizing and Rotating /Skewing Images

Images are treated as any other object when it comes to performing transformations on them like resizing, rotating, skewing etc. You are already familiar with transforming objects using the Transformations docker Window. The same process applies for all images, be it Vector or Bitmap image.

Exporting Images

You can export CorelDRAW X8 image to a different file format. This is useful when you want an image to be visible to anyone, even if he does not have a CorelDRAW X8 compatible package. For example, if you want to use an image on a Web Site, you will need to export the image into a GIF or JPG format. In CorelDRAW X8 you can also export an image in PNG format. PDF format is widely accepted for printing and Web based applications.

In addition CorelDraw X8 includes a new features to Export a drawing to the SVG file format. Scalable Vector Graphics (SVG) is an open standard graphics file format that allows designers to put the power of vector graphics to work on the Web. Scalable Vector Graphics are described in Extensible Markup Language (XML). Graphics files have an **.svg** filename extension.

To export an SVG file, do this:

1. Click File menu and choose Export....

2. In the Export dialog box, select the folder in which you want to save the image in the Save in: drop down menu.

3. Choose the file format in which you want to export the image, in the Saves as type: drop down menu.

4. Click the Scalable vector graphics to save the file.

5. Type a name for your file in the File name: text field and click Export.

6. SVG Export dialog appears as shown in Figure 11.19.

7. From the **Encoding Method**: list choose any one of the following list.

   - Let you save the drawing as a Scalable Vector Graphic (SWG) bitmap. This preserves the appearance of the drawing when you import it into an office application

   - Unicode-UTF-8 — It is a smaller file size. This is the default encoding method.

   - Unicode-UTF-16 — It is a bigger file size.

8. Choose one of the following options from the **Styling options**: drop-down list.

   - Internal style sheet — lets you embed the style sheet in the Scalable Vector Graphics file by using the Class attribute.

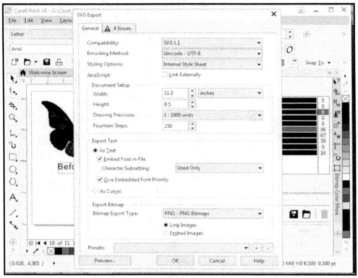

Figure 11.19 SVG Export dialog box

   - Presentation attributes — lets you specify attributes directly in an element in the exported file.

   - External CSS — creates an external cascading style sheet file and links it to the Scalable Vector Graphics file.

- If you select **Link externally** check box in the JavaScript area. Java script related to overturn and can be saved to a separate file.

9. In the **Document Setup area**, enter a value in the **Width:** spin box, and **Height:** spin box.

10. In the **Drawing Precision:** drop-down list, select the drawing precision defined as a ratio of units.

11. In the **Fountain Steps:** box, type the number of fill steps to export. (i.e. the shades of color that makes up the appearance of a fountain fill.)

12. In the **Export text** area, enable one of the following options:

- As **Text** — lets you export text as editable characters, known as single character in a font. You can also Enable the **Embed font in file** check box. Choose which fonts you want to embed from the Character sub-setting list box.

- As **Curves** — lets you export text as curves. You can also Enable the Give embedded font priority check box.

13. In the **Bitmap Export type:** drop-down list, choose JPEG, GIF, or PNG file format to export and enable one of the following options.

- **Link images** save each bitmap as a separate file that is linked to the SVG file.

- **Embed images** embeds each bitmap in the SVG file.

14. Choose a preset from the **Presets:** list box.

15. Click preview to preview the exported file. To preview the SVG file, you can use the Corel SVG viewer installed with the application. Otherwise the file can be seen in the Internet Explorer.

CHAPTER 12

Page Layout

Introduction

CorelDRAW X8 allows you to specify the size, orientation, unit of scale and background of the page of drawing. You can customize and display page grids and guidelines to help you to organize objects and place them exactly where you want. For example, if you are designing a newsletter, you can set the dimensions of the pages and create guidelines for positioning columns and heading text. When you are laying out an advertisement, you can align graphics and advertisement copy along guidelines and arrange graphic elements within a grid. Rulers can help you position grids, guidelines, and objects along a scale using units of your choosing. Also, you can add and delete pages of the document.

Layout Styles

CorelDRAW lets you choose a preset layout style for a drawing. You can choose the layout style depending on the nature of project you are working on. For example, to design a book, click on the Book style. Other options available in CorelDRAW are Booklet, Tent Card, Side-fold card and Top-fold card. In a multi page document, you can set whether you want the page to appear face to face or not.

To set layout styles for the drawing window, do this:

1. Click the **L**ayout menu and choose **P**age Setup… . The **Options** dialog box appears as shown in Figure 12.1.
2. Click on **Layout** in the left side of the **Options** dialog box.
3. In the **Document** list of categories, choose a layout style from the **La**y**out**: list box.
4. Check the **F**acing **pages** check box, if you want the left and right pages to face each other.
5. Click the **Start on**: list box and choose **Left side** to start the document on a left facing page. Click the **Right side** to start the document on a right facing page. The **Start on**: list box is highlighted only if the Layout chosen is **Full page** or **Book** style.

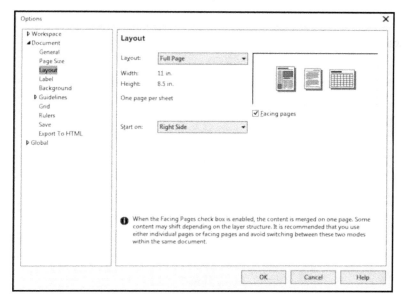

Figure 12.1 Layout tab in the Options dialog box

Define Page Size

There are two options for specifying a page size: choosing a preset page size and creating your own. If a preset page size does not meet your needs, you can create a custom page size by specifying a drawing's dimensions. The easiest way to define the page size is to click on a blank part of the Drawing area with pick tool. You can use this Property Bar to define the size and orientation of the page, as well as many other attributes. (See Figure 12.2)

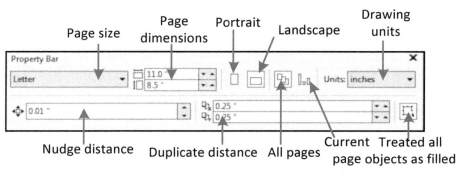

Figure 12.2 Property Bar

Setting the Size

To set the page size, do this:

1. Click <u>L</u>ayout menu and choose <u>P</u>age Setup... .
2. Click on **Page Size** in the left side of the **Options** dialog box, which appears as shown in Figure 12.3.

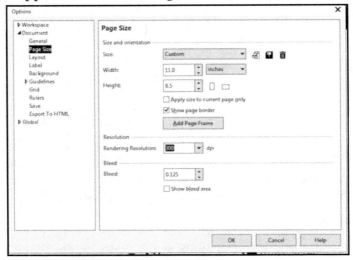

Figure 12.3 Page Size tab in the Options dialog box

3. In the **Size and Orientation** section:
4. Choose a page size from the <u>S</u>ize: list box to choose a preset page size. It you choose custom page size type values in the <u>W</u>idth: and H<u>ei</u>ght: boxes.
5. Click the **Landscape** or the **Portrait** button, to set the page orientation.
6. Set the page size and orientation for an individual page in a multipage document, enable the **Apply size to current page <u>o</u>nly** check box.
7. Display the page border to enable the S<u>h</u>ow **page border** check box.
8. To add a frame around the page, click <u>A</u>dd **Page frame** button.
9. In the **Resolution** area:
10. Choose a resolution from the **Rendering Resol<u>u</u>tion:** list box:

11. To set a bleed limit. Enable the **Show bleed area** check box, and type a value in the **Bleed** box. Bleed refers to the part of the image that extends beyond the printable area. Setting bleed limit ensures that the image fits right inside the page edges.

12. After you define your custom size, you can save the page definition so that you can use it again. To save your custom page setting, Click on the **Save** button. The **Custom Page Type** dialog box appears as shown in Figure 12.4. Provide a name for your page definition.

13. Click **OK**.

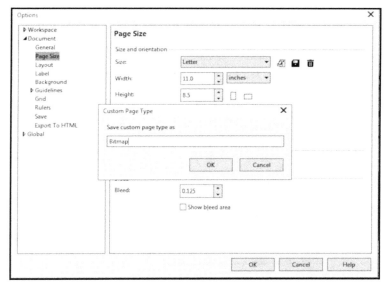

Figure 12.4 Custom Page Type dialog box

Inserting Pages

You can have more than one page in a publication. These pages can either define properties such as page size for a selected page or for all pages.

To insert pages in a publication, do this:

1. Click on the **Layout** menu, and choose **Insert Page…** . The **Insert Page…** dialog box appears as shown in Figure 12.5.

2. Specify how many pages you want to insert in the **Number of pages**: list box.

3. In the P<u>l</u>ace: section, click the <u>B</u>efore or <u>A</u>fter radio button to specify where you want place the new page(s) to appear.

4. Click the up and down arrow to choose the **Existing <u>P</u>age**: list box, to insert page number.

5. In the **Page Size** section:

6. Select size for the new page in the <u>S</u>ize: drop-down list.

7. To specify width and height of the current page, select the <u>W</u>idth: and H<u>e</u>ight: list box.

8. Click the **Portrait** radio button to transform page layout to portrait type that is pages that are taller than they are wide.

9. Click the **Landscape** radio button. To transform the page layout to landscape type that has pages that are wider than they are tall.

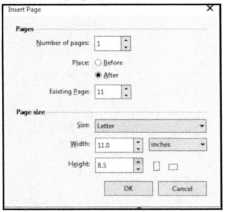

Figure 12.5 Insert Page dialog box

10. Select any unit of measurement for your page from Drawing Units drop-down list.

11. Click **OK** button.

After you insert pages, you can move from page to page by clicking the page tabs at the bottom of the CorelDRAW window.

The pages inserted can be renamed according to your requirement for easy reference and can also be deleted.

To delete a page, do this:

1. Click the <u>L</u>ayout menu and choose <u>D</u>elete Page.... The **Delete Page** dialog box appears as shown in Figure 12.6.

2. In the **Delete page**: list box, type the page number of the page you want to delete.

3. To delete multiple pages, click the **Through to page**: list box, and set the page number up to which you want to delete, in the list box.

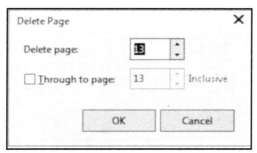

Figure 12.6 Delete Page dialog box

To rename a page, do this:

1. Move to the page which you want to rename.

2. Click the **Layout** menu and choose **Rename Page**…. The **Rename Page** dialog box appears as shown in Figure 12.7.

3. In the **Page name**: box, type the new name for the page. The current page will be renamed with this new name. Click OK.

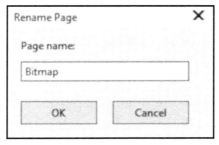

Figure 12.7 Rename Page dialog box

Specifying Background Color

You can specify the background color of a page. You can apply a solid color for background if you want a uniform background to the page or you can even apply a bitmap image as a background for your page.

To apply background color, do this:

1. Click **Layout** menu and choose **Page Background**… .

2. Click the **Background** in the left side of the **Options** dialog box as shown in Figure 12.8.

3. Click the **S**olid radio button.

4. Click the Color picker and choose a color from the drop down list.

5. Click **OK**.

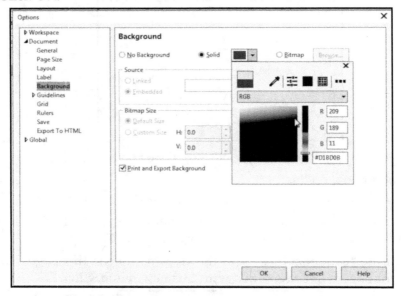

Figure 12.8 Background tab in the Options dialog box

To apply a bitmap image as background, do this:

1. In the **Options** dialog box (See Figure 12.9), click the **B**itmap radio button.

2. Click **Bro**w**se**... button. The **Import** dialog box appears.

3. Locate the file where the bitmap image file is stored.

4. If you choose **L**inked option, the changes you do in the source file will be reflected in the bitmap image background.

5. If you choose **E**mbedded, the changes made in the source file will not be reflected.

6. If you want the background to be printable and exportable, enable the **P**rint and Export Background check box.

7. Click on the **D**efault Size, to let CorelDRAW X8 tile or crop the image to fit the page.

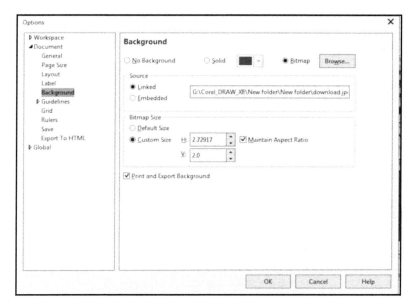

Figure 12.9 Setting bitmap as background

8. Click on <u>C</u>ustom Size to specify the dimensions of the bitmapped image. Type values in the <u>H</u>: and <u>V</u>: boxes.

9. If you want to specify non-proportional height and width values, disable the <u>M</u>aintain Aspect Ratio check box.

10. Click OK button.

To remove a background, do this:

1. Click the <u>L</u>ayout menu and choose Page <u>B</u>ackground....

2. Click the <u>N</u>o Background radio button.

Going to specific pages

To go to a specific page, do this:

1. Click the <u>L</u>ayout menu and choose <u>G</u>o to Page... . The Go To Page dialog appears as shown in Figure 12.10.

2. In the Go To Page dialog box, choose the specified page from the <u>G</u>o to page: list box and click OK.

3. *Alternatively*, you can move to a specific page, by pressing at the page tab located in the bottom left of the CorelDRAW window.

4. The facilities provided by the page tab are also known as Document Navigator and are given in Table 12.1.

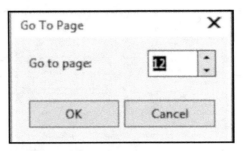

Figure 12.10 Go To Page dialog box

Table 12.1 The Buttons in Document Navigator

Name	Description
⏮ .First Page	To moves to the first page in the document.
◀ . Forward one	To move forward one page.
▶ .Back one	To move back one page.
▶⏸ .Last Page	To move to the last page in the document.
Page 2	To choose a specific page number say to go to page 2
+	Click left + (plus) button to add page at the beginning, and right + (plus) button to add page at the end.

Working with Tables

A table provides a structured layout that lets you present text or images within a drawing. You can draw a table, or you can create a table from paragraph text. You can easily change the look of a table by modifying the table properties and formatting. In addition, because tables are objects, you can manipulate them in various ways.

Adding Tables

With CorelDRAW, you can add a table to a drawing to create a structured layout for text and images. You can draw a table, or you can create a table from existing text.

To create a table to a drawing, do this:

1. Click the <u>T</u>able tool icon in the Toolbox.

2. Type values in the **Rows and columns** boxes on the property bar.

3. The value you type in the top portion specifies the number of rows; the value you type in the bottom portion specifies the number of columns.

4. Drag diagonally to draw the table. Or

5. You can create a table by clicking the <u>T</u>able menu and choose <u>C</u>reate New Table... .

6. The **Create New Table** dialog box appears as shown in Figure 12.11.

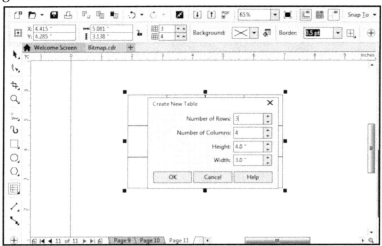

Figure 12.11 Create New Table dialog box

7. Click the **Number of Rows**: in the list box.

8. Click the **Number of Columns**: in the list box.

9. Click the **Height:** and **Width:** of the table in the list box.

10. After applying the desired setting click the OK button.

Selecting, moving and navigating table components

You must select a table, rows, columns, or cells before you insert rows or columns, change the table border properties, add a background fill color, or edit other table properties. You can move selected rows and columns to a new location in a table. You can also copy or cut a row or column from one table and paste it in another table. In addition, you can move from one table cell to another when editing the table cell text, and you can set the tab order for moving around a table.

To select a table, do this:

1. To select the Table, click the **Table** icon in the Toolbox.
2. Click the **T**able menu highlight **S**elect. A sub menu appears, select **T**able.
3. The entire table gets selected with line appears. Or
4. With the Table pointer, hover over the upper-left corner of the table until a diagonal arrow appears and then click as shown in Figure 12.12.

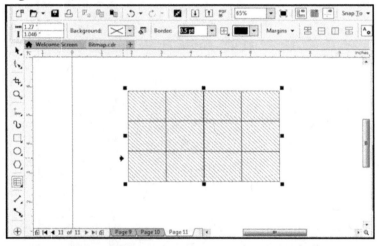

Figure 12.12 Selecting a entire table by clicking the upper-left corner of the table

To select a row, do this:

1. Click the **Table** icon in the Toolbox, and then click the table the table gets selected.
2. Click the **T**able menu highlight **S**elect. A sub menu appears, select **R**ow.
3. The entire row gets selected with line appears. Or

With the Table tool pointer, hover over the table border to the left of the row you want to select. When a horizontal arrow appears, click the border to select the row as shown in Figure 12.13.

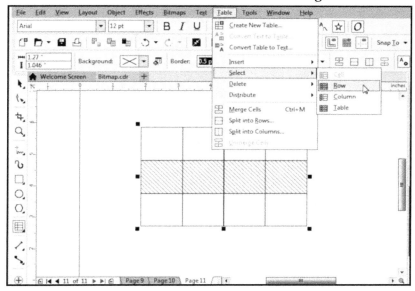

Figure 12.13 Selecting Row by Select command in the Table menu

To select a column, do this:

1. Click the Table icon in the Toolbox, and then click a table. The table gets selected.

2. Click the **T**able menu highlight **S**elect. A sub menu appears, select **C**olumn.

3. The entire row gets selected with line appears. Or

   With the Table tool pointer, hover over the top border of the column you want to select. When a vertical arrow appears, click the border to select the column as shown in Figure 12.14.

To move a table row or column, do this:

1. Select the row or column you want to move.

2. Drag the row or column to another location in the table.

Inserting and Deleting table rows and columns

You can insert and delete the rows and columns in a table.

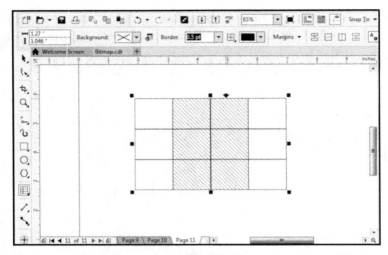

Figure 12.14 Selecting column by clicking top edge of the border

To insert a table row, do this:

1. Select a row in the table.

2. Click the <u>T</u>able menu highlight <u>I</u>nsert. A sub menu appears choose Row <u>A</u>bove or Row <u>B</u>elow.

3. The row will be inserted above or below the selected row. Or

   To insert multiple rows above or below the selection, click the <u>T</u>able menu highlight <u>I</u>nsert and choose Insert <u>R</u>ows... .

4. The **Insert Rows** dialog box appears as shown in Figure 12.15.

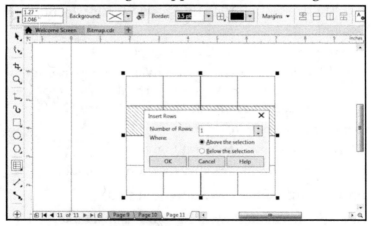

Figure 12.15 Insert Rows dialog box

5. Type the value in the Number of Rows: list box.

6. Click the desired radio button Above the selection or Below the selection in the Where: radio button.

7. The Row is inserted Above the Selection as shown in Figure 12.15.

When you use either the **Row above** command or the **Row below** command from the **Table** and choose **Insert** menu, the number of rows that are inserted depends on how many rows you have selected. For example, if you have selected two rows, then two rows are inserted in the table.

To insert a table column, do this:

1. Select a column in the table.

2. Click the Table menu highlight Insert and choose Column Left or Column Right.

3. The column will be inserted left or right of the selected column. Or

   To insert multiple columns to the left or right of the selected column, click the Table menu highlight Insert and choose Insert Columns... .

4. The Insert columns dialog box appears as shown in Figure 12.16.

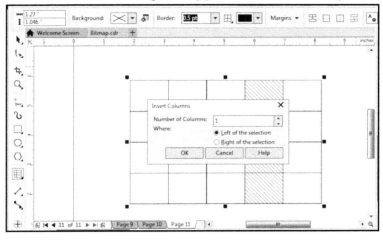

Figure 12.16 Insert Columns dialog box

5. Click the desired radio button Left of the selection or Right of the selection in Where: radio button.

6. The Column is inserted at the left of the selection as shown in Figure 12.16.

To delete a row, do this:

1. Select the row you want to delete.
2. Click the Table menu highlight Delete and then choose Row.
3. The selected row will be deleted.

To delete a column, do this:

1. Select the column you want to delete.
2. Click the Table menu highlight Delete and then choose Column.
3. The selected column will be deleted.

Resizing table cell, row and column

You can resize table cell, row, and column. Alternatively, if you changed the size of a row or column, you can distribute them to make all the rows or columns the same size.

To resize table cell, row/column, do this:

1. Select the table with the Pick tool.
2. Select the cell, row or column that you want to resize.
3. On the Property bar, type values in the Height and Width box. (See Figure 12.17)

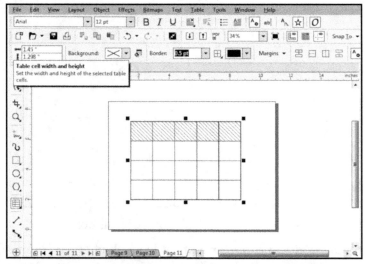

Figure 12.17 Resizing the row and column in the property bar

To distribute table rows, do this:

1. Select the table rows that you want to distribute.

2. Click the <u>T</u>able menu highlight Dist<u>r</u>ibute. A sub menu appears, select <u>R</u>ows Evenly

3. The selected rows are the same height as shown in Figure 12.18.

4. The selected rows distribute evenly.

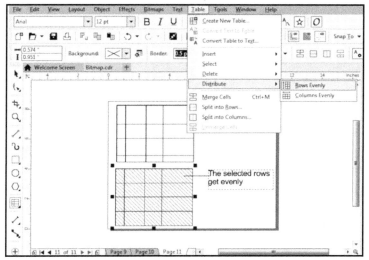

Figure 12.18   The selected rows gets same height as shown below the table

To distribute table columns, do this:

1. Select the table columns that you want to distribute.

2. Click the <u>T</u>able menu highlight Dist<u>r</u>ibute. A sub menu appears, select <u>C</u>olumns Evenly.

3. The selected columns are the same width as shown in Figure 12.19.

4. The selected columns distribute evenly.

Working with text in tables

You can easily add text to table cells. The text in table cells is treated as paragraph text. Therefore, you can modify the table text as you would other paragraph text. For example, you can change the font, add bullets, or indents.

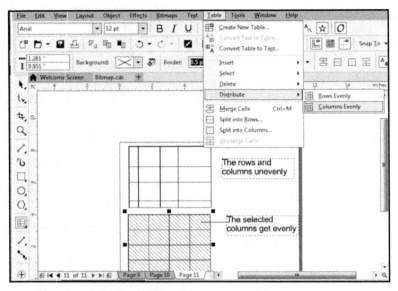

Figure 12.19 The selected columns gets same width as shown below the table

To type text in a table cell, do this:

1. Click the **Table** tool.
2. Click a cell.
3. Type text in the cell as shown in Figure 12.20.

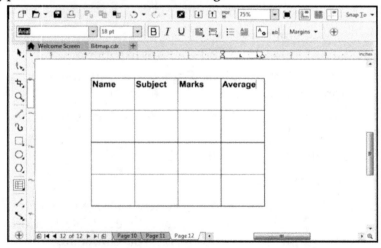

Figure 12.20 Entering text in a table cell

To automatically resize table cells when you type, do this:

1. Click the Pick tool, and then click the table.

2. Click Options on the property bar, and enable Automatically resize cells while typing check box as shown in Figure 12.21.

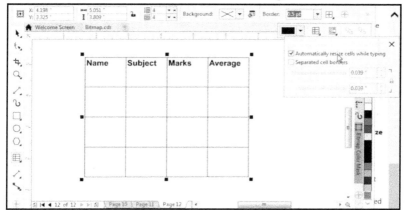

Figure 12.21 Resize the cells while typing in the property bar

Converting tables to text

You can convert the table text to paragraph text, if you no longer want the table text to appear in a table.

To convert a table to text, do this:

1. Click the Table tool, and then click the table.

2. Click Table menu highlight Convert Table to Text... .

3. The Convert Table to Text dialog box appears as shown in Figure 12.22.

4. In the Separate cell text with: area, choose one of the following options:

   Commas: It replaces each column with a comma and replaces each row with a paragraph marker.

   Tabs: It replaces each column with a tab and replaces each row with a paragraph marker.

   Paragraphs: It replaces each column with a paragraph marker.

   User Defined: It replaces each column with a specified character and replaces each row with a paragraph marker.

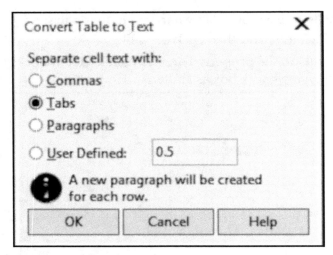

Figure 12.22 Convert Table to Text dialog box

5. Click the desired options and then click OK button. For example, here to select the **Tabs** options, you will notice the table convert to text in between commas as shown in Figure 12.23.

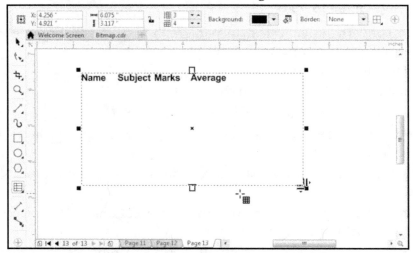

Figure 12.23 The Table convert to paragraph text

Merging and Splitting Cells

Use the Merge Cells feature to join multiple cells. Similarly, use the split feature to separate cells.

To merge the cells, do this:

1. Select the cells to be merged.

2. Click the **T**able menu and choose **M**erge **C**ells. Alternatively press Ctrl+M keys together.

3. The selected two cells get merged as shown in Figure 12.24.

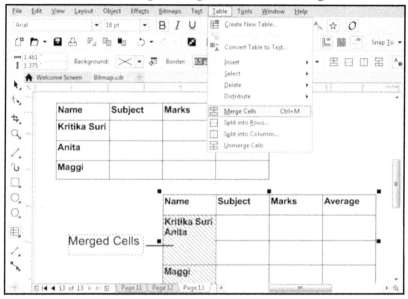

Figure 12.24 By selecting Merge command and the cells get merged

To Unmerge the cells, do this:

1. Select the cell that you want to unmerge.

2. Click **T**able menu and choose **U**nmerge cells.

3. The unmerge cells get merged as shown in Figure 12.25.

To Split table rows horizontally, do this:

1. Click the **Table** tool.

2. Select the row that you want to divide into two.

3. Click the **T**able menu and choose **S**plit into **R**ows... .

4. The **Split Cells** dialog box shows number of row as shown in Figure 12.26.

5. Type a value in the **Number of rows:** box. The row gets split horizontally as shown in Figure 12.27.

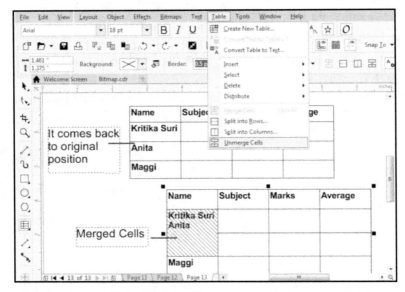

Figure 12.25 By selecting Unmerge cells it comes back to merge cells

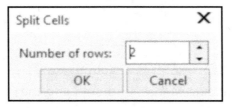

Figure 12.26 Split Cells dialog

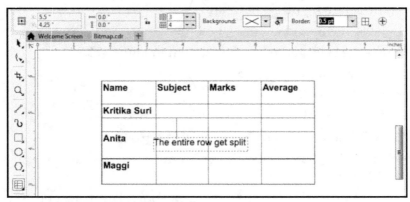

Figure 12.27 Row split horizontally

To Split table columns vertically, do this:

1. Click the **Table** tool.
2. Select the column that you want to divide into two.
3. Click the **T**able menu and choose **S**plit into Columns... .

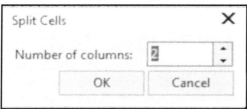

Figure 12.28   Split Cells dialog box

4. The **Split Cells** dialog box shows number of columns as shown in Figure 12.28.
5. Type a value in the **Number of columns:** box. The column gets split vertically as shown in Figure 12.29.

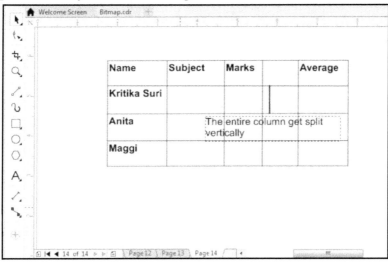

Figure 12.29   Columns split vertically

CHAPTER 13

Printing and Publishing Options

Introduction

CorelDRAW X8 comes with a full set of printer options to make it easy for printing business cards, labels, and other odd-sized output. In CorelDRAW X8, you can print one or more copies of the same drawing. You can specify what to print, as well as which part of a drawing to print. For example, you can print selected vectors, bitmaps, text, or layers. Before printing a drawing, you can specify printer properties, including paper size and device options.

Selecting a Printer

To select a printer do this:

1. Click the <u>F</u>ile menu and choose <u>P</u>rint... . The **Print** dialog box appears as shown in Figure 13.1. Or press **Ctrl + P** keys together.

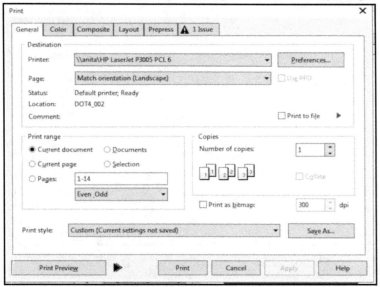

Figure 13.1 Print dialog box

2. Click the **General** Tab.
3. In the **Destination** area, choose a printer from the **Printer:** list box.

4. Choose a page size and orientation option from the **Page** list box.

5. In the **Print range** area, the options are:

    Current document:– To print all the pages in your document, click the current document radio button.

    Current Page:– To print the active page in your document, click the Current page radio button.

    Pages:– To print range of pages, say, pages 1 to 20 in a 50 page document, type the first page number and then select the desired page number in the **Pages:** radio button. Separate the numbers with hyphen like 1-20.

    In the **Pages** drop down list, select the desired pages you want.

    Documents – To print more than one document at a time click this radio button.

    Selection – To print the selected text, first select it, and then click the **Selection** radio button. This option is dimmed unless you have selected something in your document.

6. In the **Copies** area, the options are:

    Number of copies: – Specify the number of copies of the document you want to print in the number of copies list box.

    Collate – This option determines how multiple copies are printed. For example, if you have a four-page document and you want to print two copies, collating prints pages 1, 2, 3, and 4, and then prints pages 1, 2, 3, and 4 in that order. If you do not select the **Collate** check box, your two copies print in the order of two copies of page 1, followed by two copies of page 2, two copies of page 3 and so on. You will need to arrange them manually to make the sets.

7. After making changes click print button to print the document.

Using Layout Styles when Printing

CorelDRAW X8 gives you a lot of options to control how your document is printed. Using the options in layout tab of the **Print** dialog box, you define the print attributes on your document.

To specify the size and position of a print job, do this:

1. Select the object or paragraph text in the document.

2. Click the **File** menu and choose **Print...** . The **Print** dialog box appears.

3. Click the **Layout** tab property sheet appears as shown in Figure 13.2.

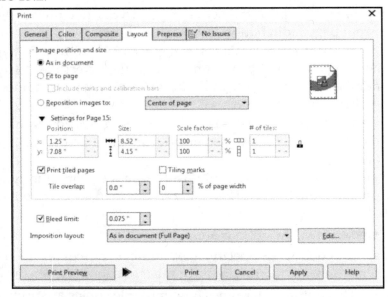

Figure 13.2 Layout tab showing As in document

4. There are three ways to treat the position and size of layout.

   As in document–Click this radio button, to print your document as it is without any modification. (See Figure 13.2)

   Fit to page–Click this radio button, to scale the image so that it fits the printable page (See Figure 13.3).

   Reposition images to:–Click this radio button to place the printed image as per your requirement. In the position, specified in the list box on the right side, adjust the Position, Size and Scale values below it (See Figure 13.4).

   - **Position:** It displays the position of your document on the left and top of the page.
   - **Size:** It displays the size of printed area (not the original document) and gives the height and width of the page.
   - **Scale factor:** It displays the scale of your printed area (not the original document) by the specified percentage.

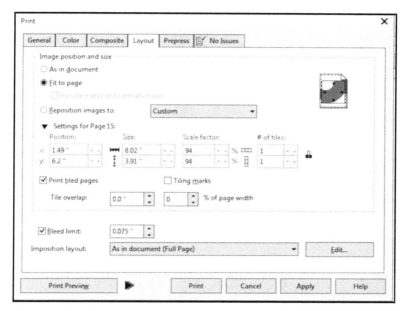

Figure 13.3 Fit to page options scales the contents to fit the page

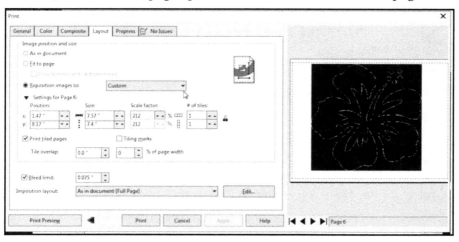

Figure 13.4 Selecting Reposition images to in the Layout tab

5. When you select as per your need of options selected in the print dialog box, you can see the small preview window at the right corner of the dialog box. Or You can quickly preview a print job by clicking the **Mini preview** button.

Tiling a Print Job

Tiling feature is useful when you want to print a drawing, which is larger than the paper your printer can print. So using this feature, CorelDRAW X8 tiles your document. You can then print these tiles and assemble them to get the document.

To tile a print job, do this:

1. Click the File menu and choose Print... .
2. Click the Layout tab.
3. Click the Print tiled pages check box. This enables you to print large print jobs on multiple sheets, or tiles, that can be assembled later to form the entire document. Type values in the list boxes.

   Tile overlap: – specify the number of inches by which to overlap tiles.

   % of page width: – specify the percentage of the page width, the tiles will occupy.

   # of tiles: – let you specify the number of horizontal and vertical tiles on the page.
4. Click the Tiling marks check box. This enable to include tiling alignment marks.
5. Click the Print Preview button as shown in Figure 13.5.
6. To Close print preview press Alt + C keys together.

Using Print Style

A print style is a set of saved printing options. Each print style is a separate file. This lets you move a print style from one machine to another, back up a print style, and keep document specific styles in the same folder as the document file.

You can select a print style or edit a print style and save such changes. You can also delete print styles.

To choose a print style, do this:

1. Click the File menu and choose Print... .
2. Choose a Print style, from the Print style: list box as CorelDRAW defaults or Browse.

To create a print style, do this:

1. Click the File menu and choose Print... . Choose General Tab.

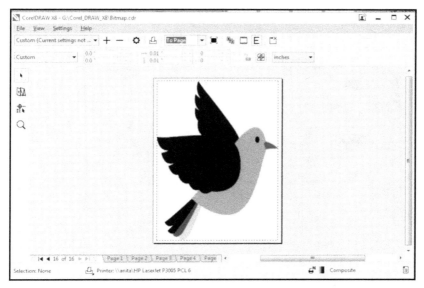

Figure 13.5 Showing Print Preview with Full page

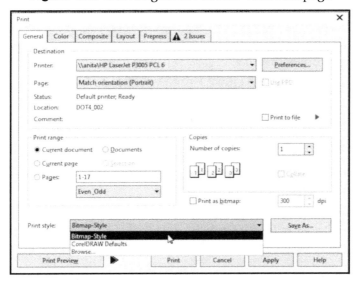

Figure 13.6 Selecting Print Style in the Print dialog box

2. Click Sa**v**e As... button, it opens Save Setting As dialog box appears as shown in Figure 13.6.

3. In Save **i**n: list box choose the drive and folder where the print style is stored as shown in Figure 13.7.

Figure 13.7 Save Setting As dialog box

4. Type a name for the style in the File name: list box. Click Save button.

To delete a print style, do this:

1. Click the File menu and chose Print Preview... .
2. Select a print style in the standard toolbar.
3. Click the Delete print style button (i.e. Minus sign (--)).

Print to a File

The Print to file option allows you to create a file that can later be downloaded to the selected output device.

To print to a file do this:

1. Click the File and choose Print... .
2. Click the General tab.
3. Click the Print to file check box. Click the flyout button and choose from the following options (See Figure 13.8).

   Single File – prints pages to a single file

   Pages to separate files – prints pages to separate files.

   Plates to separate files – prints plates to separate files.

4. Click **Print**. After taken printout:
5. Choose one of the following from the **Save as type** list box.
   - **Print file** — saves the file as a PRN file.
   - **PostScript file** — saves the file as a PS file.
6. Choose the folder where you want to save the file.
7. Type a filename in the **File name** box.
8. Click **Save**.

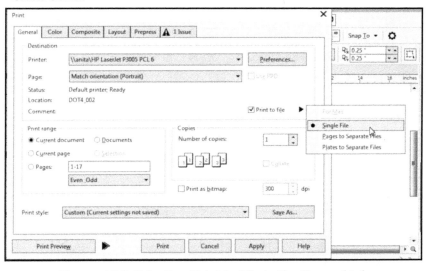

Figure 13.8 Selecting Print to File in the General tab